Prayers, Poems, Ponderings

SANDY EMMERSON

LUCIDBOOKS

Prayers, Poems, Ponderings

Copyright © 2025 by Sandy Emmerson

Published by Lucid Books in Houston, TX
www.LucidBooks.com

All rights reserved. No part of this publication may be reproduced, stored in a retrieval system, or transmitted in any form by any means, electronic, mechanical, photocopy, recording, or otherwise, without the prior permission of the publisher, except as provided for by USA copyright law.

Unless otherwise indicated, scripture quotations are taken from the (NIV) Holy Bible, New International Version®, NIV®. Copyright ©1973, 1978, 1984, 2011 by Biblica, Inc.™ Used by permission of Zondervan. All rights reserved worldwide. www.zondervan.com The "NIV" and "New International Version" are trademarks registered in the United States Patent and Trademark Office by Biblica, Inc.™

Scripture quotations marked (ESV) are taken from the ESV® Bible (The Holy Bible, English Standard Version®), copyright © 2001 by Crossway, a publishing ministry of Good News Publishers. Used by permission. All rights reserved.

Scripture quotations marked (NLT) are taken from the Holy Bible, New Living Translation, copyright ©1996, 2004, 2015 by Tyndale House Foundation. Used by permission of Tyndale House Publishers, Carol Stream, Illinois 60188. All rights reserved.

ISBN: 978-1-63296-917-0 Paperback
ISBN: 978-1-63296-918-7 Hardback
eISBN: 978-1-63296-919-4

Special Sales: Most Lucid Books titles are available in special quantity discounts. Custom imprinting or excerpting can also be done to fit special needs. Contact Lucid Books at Info@LucidBooks.com

Dedication

Since my mother was the first to encourage a love of reading and writing in me, this one is dedicated to her, Bettie Louise Gorman Sanders. Thank you for the countless ways you showed me love. I can only hope to be half as good at that.

Contents

1. Deeply 2
2. All Things 4
3. Whatever Is Good 6
4. Looking in the Right Direction 8
5. The Switch 10
6. Happiness Is a Warm Quilt 12
7. The Wind Beneath 14
8. Sharing the Load 16
9. Sunday Best 18
10. The Prince's Domain 20
11. Our Father 22
12. My Strength 24
13. The Outstretched Arm 26
14. Refuge 28
15. Inside Out 30
16. The Pitchfork 32
17. Fashion Choices 34
18. The Unlikely Hero 36
19. Encouraging Words 38
20. The Happy Alternative 40
21. A Pearl of Wisdom 42
22. The Butterflies 44
23. Stained Glass 46
24. Fully Restored 48
25. Reflection 50
26. His Hand 52

27. Quiet Beauty 54
28. Kept Promises 56
29. The Way 58
30. Underneath It All 60
31. The Unexplainable 62
32. First Family 64
33. The Butterflies 66
34. Your Light 68
35. Reaching to the Heavens 70
36. Freedom Fighters..72
37. The Masterpiece 74
38. The Most Beautiful Story 76
39. So Much More 78
40. Soul Streaming 80
41. The Discipline 82
42. On a Lighter Note 84
43. New Mercies 86
44. Tiny Seeds 88
45. Spilling Over 90
46. The Letter 92
47. Never Alone 94
48. Listening Ears 96
49. The Oaks 98
50. Serious Conversations 100
51. Running the Race 102
52. Sure-footed 104
53. Lost and Found 106
54. Tough Love 108
55. The Fortress 110
56. The Scattering of Light 112

57.	Joyful, Patient, Faithful	114
58.	Listening Ears	116
59.	Great Advice	118
60.	Fixed	120
61.	Lifted and Exalted	122
62.	Full	124
63.	Numbering Our Days	126
64.	Together	128
65.	Closer Than a Brother	130
66.	The Best Medicine	132
67.	Holding Fast	134
68.	Way Maker	136
69.	Declarations of Appreciation	138
70.	Fullness of Grace	140
71.	Be Still	142
72.	The Overseer	144
73.	Practice Meets Perfect	146
74.	Calming the Waves	148
75.	Cleaning Day	150
76.	Calming the Waves	152
77.	Night and Day	154
78.	No Eye	156
79.	In Service	158
80.	First	160
81.	Gift Giving	162
82.	First	164
83.	Good Fruit	166
84.	Philadelphia	168
85.	Jumping In	170
86.	Gift	172

87. Great Grace	174
88. The Bottom Line	176
89. The Way	178
90. Lifted and Exalted	180
91. Down in My Heart	182
92. New Things	184
93. New Things	186
94. A Light in the Darkness	188
95. The Festival	190
96. Perfect Peace	192
97. In His Hand	194
98. Up and Over	196
99. This Day	198
100. A Special Freedom	200
101. New Things	202

1.
Today's Prayer

Deeply

1 Peter 1:22, John 13:34

Dear Jesus,

I praise You for this day, a day to love our neighbors deeply as You have loved us. To do this is the fulfillment of the second commandment that You gave to us. When we fulfill this commandment, Your child John tells us that we are born of God because that is who He is. As a matter of fact, John repeats this three times. Lord, direct our minds, hearts, and actions to love one another deeply. Keep us seeking You day after day so that we can discover all of the ways You love us and generously return such favors back to others.

In Your Name Above All names, I humbly pray-

The Decision

Love is a decision
The wisest ever made
Because it is the heart of God
His Spirit on Earth portrayed.

Love is a decision
The kindest one to share
It lifts up others near and far
To let them know we care.

Love is a decision
To leave the world a better place
With a peaceful atmosphere
Of happiness and of grace.

SJ Emmerson

Who needs my love today? Write your personal prayers, ponderings or poems.

2.

Today's Prayer

All Things

Psalm 84:11, Philippians 4:13, 1 Thessalonians

Dear Jesus,

I praise You for this day. Like every day, this is a day to pray continually and be joyful for the Grace and Love exercised in answering such prayers. Your perspective of our circumstances looks vastly different from ours, so the answers may often look different than our expectations. We can rest thankfully assured, however, that our best interest is at the heart of Your answer. Lord, thank You for the sun You shine on our lives and in our hearts, a bolster to our hopeful happiness. Thank You for the shield of protection that preserves us and enables us to do all things You have planned for us to accomplish. Thank You for all things because in Your Hand, it will all work out for the best.

In Your Name Above All names, I humbly pray-

Behind the Clouds

Even when the darkest clouds
Tumble and roll on by
The sun is shining brightly
A little Higher in the sky.

Even as the wind roars past
With cruel, destructive hands
God is busy clearing a path
For new and exciting plans.

Even though the icy rains
Chill straight into the bone
His Shelter waits with warming love
In this storm, we are not alone.

SJ Emmerson

Sunshine on a cloudy day. Is there anything better? How can I share some joy today? Write your personal prayers, ponderings or poems.

3.
Today's Prayer

Whatever Is Good

Philippians 4:8

Dear Jesus,

I praise You for this day, a day to think about the good things You have provided. You have set into motion things that are true, noble, just, pure, lovely, and admirable. Why would we dwell on ugly, stressful, negative objects when we can turn our thoughts to that which is excellent or praiseworthy? Happy thoughts feed happy hearts. It is all there for the thinking. Lord, when our thoughts turn sour, please adjust our eyes to see one of Your beautiful designs in Creation both inside and outside of these Image made bodies of ours.

In Your Name Above All names, I humbly pray-

The Wonders of Today

Porch time on a day
A cool breeze before the dawn
Glances at a star-filled sky
Before the night is gone.

A grandchild reaching for a hug
A pansy's friendly smile
Updates from a special one
The chrysanthemum's sassy style.

The happiness of those we love
A restful afternoon
Coffee's early morning scent
A silver half-full moon.

Wonders come in many shapes
Sizes range from great to small
Whatever wonders come our way
We can thank Our Father for them all.

SJ Emmerson

Which of my blessings will I actually write down in a journal?
Write your personal prayers, ponderings or poems.

4.
Today's Prayer
Looking in the Right Direction

Micah 7:7, Isaiah 40:30-31, Psalm 22:19

Dear Jesus,

I praise You for this day, a day to be on the lookout for Your direction and Your help. It is not always easy to see Your signposts as the weather down here at times prevents a clear view. At times, the hail is falling at such speeds, we just have to hunker down and close our eyes to prevent injury. Being the Good Father that You are, though, You gave us a built in route straight to You from the inside out. We can always pray. In fact, sometimes it is even a more effective form of communication. You will be eagerly waiting to hear from us. We need only to wait until the optimal time for You to lift us up and carry us to the next assignment. Lord, tilt our heads and point our eyes, both the exterior and the interior, in Your direction even if our vision is obstructed. Help us remember that Yours never is. Surround us with Your protection as we wait for our Eagle flight.

In Your Name Above All names, I humbly pray-

The Masquerade

Fear is only a masquerade
A ghost behind a mask.
It is a master of distraction
To shield us from finishing worthy tasks.

The only time fear can hurt us
Is if we let it come inside.
When we dare to look it in its eyes
It turns quickly and runs to hide.

A product of a fallen world
Fear is borne of hateful deceit.
But our trust in Heaven's Loving Heart
Can ensure its final defeat.

SJ Emmerson

What directions, if any, did I receive today? Write your personal prayers, ponderings or poems.

5.
Today's Prayer
The Switch

Philippians 2:14-15, 1 Thessalonians 5:16-18

Dear Jesus,

I praise You for this day, a day to switch our attitude from complaining about what we do to being thankful in all we do. Instead of grumbling, we will rejoice. We will choose to pray about our perceived misfortunes rather than grumble about them. We will give thanks in all circumstances in place of worrying, fretting, and whining. Lord, remind us that everything is made beautiful by Your touch. Please grant us the faith and vision to perceive Your Lovingkindness.

In Your Name Above All names, I humbly pray-

The Switch

We can't always choose our circumstance
But we can choose our attitude,
As it can switch out a gloomy day
For a bright and cloudless mood.

The practice of positive thinking
Comes with many fine benefits
Like hope in the best of outcomes
And joyful, peace-loving spirits.

We may need some help in succeeding
In switching to a new mindset
But our Help is always waiting
When we turn to our souls' Advocate.

SJ Emmerson

What situations cause me to need a change of attitude? Have I prayed about it? Write your personal prayers, ponderings or poems.

6.
Today's Prayer

Happiness Is a Warm Quilt

Psalm 147:3, 2 Corinthians 4:8

Dear Jesus,

I praise You for this day, a day to be thankful for Your comfort and healing. You have wrapped a warm quilt stitched with knowledge of Your comfort and care. You heal the broken hearted and bind the wounds of those who are hurting. Though we may be knocked down, we will not be crushed. Lord, when our lives seem to be bleeding out, please remind us that You will bind it together at the perfect time. You are, after all, the Great Physician.

In Your Name Above All names, I humbly pray-

The Quilt

Just like a handmade patchwork quilt
God's comfort warmly covers us.
His Spirit designs the patchwork shapes
That are stitched together with our trust.

The largest piece is unfailing love
Surrounded by His mercy and His grace.
The round, white patch represents His peace
And the heart His kind embrace.

The Royal blue velvet prayer piece
Stands for our answered prayers
The Cross shaped form, His sacrifice
And forgiveness He graciously shares.

Although the earthly winters
Bring sorrow and certain woe
We're never without His comfort
And His Love that overflows.

SJ Emmerson

When was I wrapped in God's quilt of comfort and care? Did I share that information? What are your prayers, poems, or ponderings?

7.

Today's Prayer

The Wind Beneath

Matthew 19:26, Isaiah 43:19, Acts 4:36-37

Dear Jesus,

I praise You for this day. It is a day to celebrate and remember all of the seemingly impossible mountains in our lives that You and Your messengers have helped us to climb. You have truly made ways in the wilderness and rivers in the deserts for us. You have sent Your love and grace through the lives of others who have encouraged us and helped us bear our burdens. They have been the steady wind beneath our fledgling wings. We might never have been able to fulfill the busy agendas You wrote for us many years ago if it weren't for the pathways You cleared for us and the many special people who cheered for us along the way. Thank You, Lord, for all blessings. They make the seemingly impossible possible.

In Your Name Above All names, I humbly pray-

Sunflower Friends

Everyone should be so lucky
To have a sunflower friend.
A friend who extends a helping hand
One on whom others can depend.
Her head frequently tilted up
To Heaven's gracious gifts
Always looking to find another
Who can use a special lift.
Spreading seeds of kind goodwill
She blesses those she meets
Finding joy in all that comes her way
Caring deeply for those in need.

SJEmmerson

What are your own prayers, poems, or ponderings?

8.
Today's Prayer

Sharing the Load

Galatians 6:5

Dear Jesus,

I praise You for this day, a day to share the burdens of one another. You certainly did everything You could to relieve our burdens while You were here on this planet— You healed the sick, the suffering, the afflicted, even the dead. You made a way for us to have an abundant, eternal life. In Heaven, You continue to intercede for Your children. Lord, point us in the right direction, and grant us the right resources to help those who need a helping hand. Nothing we can ever do will be enough to repay You, but when You are involved, our efforts will serve their good purposes.

In Your Name Above All names, I humbly pray-

Fragrant Offerings

Praise that comes from deep within
Offered sincerely from the heart
Is a true, unblemished offering
A sacrificial work of art.

Acts of kindness without return
Given from compassion and from care
Are worship in its highest form
A strong, well-crafted prayer.

A loving gift, devotion's child
Tender, secret sacrifice
An offering dipped from God's own well
Is of value beyond any price.

SJ Emmerson

How can I serve someone today? What are your prayers, poems, or ponderings?

9.

Today's Prayer

Sunday Best

Colossians 3:12, 2 Corinthians 6:6, 1 Corinthians 13:4

Dear Jesus,

I praise You for this day, a day not only to soak in Your blessings, but also a day to be a blessing to our neighbors. As Your children, we should select only the most royal of clothing before we venture into our day. Our hearts are clothed to the hilt when we choose to clad them in loving compassion, kindness, humility, gentleness, and patience. We much more accurately deliver the message of Your Kingdom as a result of such choices in attire. Lord, direct us to make elegant selections in our heart's wardrobe so that others will see Your beauty in our appearance. It always makes for a much richer day.

In Your Name Above All names, I humbly pray-

The Strongest Weapons

Some think the strongest weapons
Are made to annihilate
But the secret of real power
Is diffusing anger and defeating hate.

When prayer is in our quiver
We tap into an Omnipotent Source
Known to move the highest mountains
With a supernatural force.

Patient, compassionate spirits
Are most effective in such fights
And Love that conquers evil
Quells the darkness, leading to Light.

SJ Emmerson

How can I bless someone today? What are your prayers, poems, or ponderings?

10.

Today's Prayer

The Prince's Domain

John 14:27

Dear Jesus,

I praise You for this day, a day to be thankful for Your peace that passes human understanding. Unlike the peace the world offers, Your peace is not contingent on human circumstances. It is available through the work of Your Spirit at work within our hearts and minds. Your peace is able to broach the gap between death on Earth and life in Heaven. Lord, we can't understand how You do Your work, but we certainly can perceive the difference It makes in our lives. Guide us to sow Your seeds of peace through our thoughts, words, and actions. We are only human, but You are most capable of multiplying our efforts in extraordinary ways.

In Your Name Above All names, I humbly pray-

The Dove

God promises His peace of mind
To those who trust in Him
He offers daily mercies
And seeks to save rather than to condemn.

His peace cannot be bought or sold
We find it in His Word
In prayer and in quiet times
When in our hearts His Voice is heard.

He sent His Son, The Prince of Peace
To demonstrate His Love
With an offer to exchange our fears
For the peace of Heaven Above.

SJ Emmerson

Is there any war still raging in my heart? What are your prayers, poems, or ponderings?

11.

Today's Prayer

Our Father

1John 4:8, Colossians 3:14

Dear Jesus,

I praise You today for Your Love which is identical to the love of Our Father. As a matter of fact, Our Father is the Spirit of Love. He knitted together all that is through You and His Love binds us all together. Thank You, Lord, for giving us the opportunity and privilege to be adopted into Your family and bound by Your Great Grace and Magnificent Mercy.

In Your Name Above All Names, I humbly pray-

What Greater Love?

What greater hope can we ever hold
Than the assurance of Heaven's home
Where the God of grace and mercy reigns
And welcomes His children as His own?

What greater joy can there ever be
Than to know Christ left His throne above
To replace the darkness game, scorn
And hang upon a rugged cross in our hearts
With light and endless love?

What greater grace can be assigned
Than to open a hand to an angry fist
That He may lead us back to Heaven's home
And our transgressions be dismissed?

What greater Love can ever be
Than to endure hatred, shame, and scorn
Then hang upon a rugged cross
That our hearts might be reborn?

SJ Emmerson

How am I honoring God's family? What are your prayers, poems, and ponderings?

12.

Today's Prayer

My Strength

Psalm 18:1, Matthew 22:33-38

Dear Jesus,

I praise You for today just because You are my God and I love You. You are my strength, the very maker of the Heavens and Earth. You have planned a host of goodness for each one of us. You are the One able to lift our spirit up on eagles' wings when it falls low. You give me peace that passes all understanding in the hardest of times. If we ask You for something, You are there to listen to the request and give back what is best for me. We always find You when we seek You with our whole hearts. When we knock on Your door, You are there to answer, and You rejoice that we chose to come to You. Lord, help us love You from the inside out with all our hearts, soul, and minds.

In Your Name Above All names, I humbly pray-

The Eagle

Flying high above the common ground
The eagle contemplates
The wisest plan of action
To help the world's sad and fallen state.

His courage fuels his fearlessness
To stand against his foe
And defend inspired visions
Though they defy the current flow.

He comes prepared despite its cost
And rises on the storm.
He looks to new horizons
Ready to successfully perform.

He searches out the best in all
And teaches some to soar.
With a servant's heart he leads the rest
To a life much better than before.

SJ Emmerson

Who do I need to lift up today? What are your prayers, poems, or ponderings?

13.

Today's Prayer

The Outstretched Arm

Amos 4:13, Genesis 1, Jeremiah 32:7

Dear Jesus,

I praise You for this day, a day to be thankful for Your Power and Your Presence. With Your infinite might and outstretched Arm, You set in motion the heavens and the earth. Your very breath breathed life into us all and blessed us. Nothing is impossible for You. You also gave us a spirit of power and love along with a sound mind to make good judgements when we chose to believe in You. Although we live in a fallen world, You work all things for the good of those who love you and have been called according to Your purpose. Thank You, Lord, for a love big enough to create the heavens and, yet, graceful enough to call us Your children. Help us to find Your outstretched Arm in all circumstances of our lives.

In Your Name Above All names, I humbly pray-

Mountains to Molehills

We can move a massive mountain
When we place our faith in God
His strength is monumental
While our strength is weak and flawed.

His Power brings the dead to life
He can supply our every need
He's the One whose Mighty Spirit
Makes us able to succeed.

We sometimes think we're powerless
In the face of adversity
But waiting faithfully for Him to help
Can herald a victory.

SJ Emmerson

Have I blocked God's power by insisting to solve problems without the Best Advice? What are your prayers, poems, or ponderings?

14.

Today's Prayer

Refuge

John 10:4, Nahum 1:7, Psalm 37:39-40

Dear Jesus,

I praise You for this day, a day to take refuge in You because You are our stronghold against all of the anger, hate, and discord of this world. You know the names of those of us who trust You, who live with You in their hearts. You seek to gather us near You for protection. You have always walked a few steps ahead to make a way through our deserts and help us cross our rivers. Lord, we know how treacherous the roads on this planet can be. Grant us the good sense to slip away from fretting and slip into the safe haven of Your Word and have a great conversation with You through our prayers. We know You are waiting enthusiastically for us to arrive.

In Your Name Above All names, I humbly pray-

A Different Peace

Peace beyond our understanding
Is always ours to take
When we seek His Precious Spirit
Shared for our goodness' sake.

It comes differently than worldly peace
Not through money, power, or fame
It doesn't come to the one who is first
But to the one of least acclaim.

Peace comes in acts of kindness
Through debts we disregard
Through caring sincerely for others
Through the One Divinely Perfect heart.

SJ Emmerson

Am I too stubborn to hunker down in prayer and His Word when I need refuge? What are your prayers, poems, or ponderings?

15.

Today's Prayer

Inside Out

Luke 16:15, 1 Samuel 16:7, Ephesians 1:4,5

Dear Jesus,

I praise You for this day, a day to remember that You can see through our exteriors and into our hearts. Before time began, You loved us and chose us to be Your children. Even though our hearts and lives will never be perfect on our own, You still made provisions for both forgiveness and improvements paid for by Your ultimate sacrifice. All we have to do is open our hearts and minds to You. Lord, thank You for seeing our hearts through the eyes of Love. Please remind us to seek Your Spirit in all of our human circumstances. Feel free to sweep out the cobwebs from inside our souls so that Your Light can shine through us and out into this world. What we need in this world more than anything is Your Lovingkindness to shine brightly from our lives.

In Your Name Above All names, I humbly pray-

God's Eyes

God's eyes see passed the obvious
To deep within our hearts.
His view spans every moment lived
With all life's stops and starts.

They gaze on us with tenderness
From a Father's point of view.
Though He knows our thoughts and motives
He still loves us through and through.

We can't hide from such keen vision
It is foolish to even try
But we can always seek His guidance
And stand willing to comply.

SJ Emmerson

Lovingkindness-Is this what people see in me? What prayers, poems, or ponderings do you have?

16.
Today's Prayer

The Pitchfork

1 Thessalonians 5:16-18, Philippians 4:4

Dear Jesus,

I praise You for this day! It is a day to use Your three-pronged pitchfork to help us bale all of the day's hay successfully. We must rejoice always, pray continually, and give You thanks in all circumstances. We can rejoice always because whatever Satan means for our harm, You are able to turn to our advantage. You are, after all, the One who exchanges our ashes for joy. Our continual prayers are the life jackets that prevent us from drowning in the devil's dirty water. Giving thanks to You is such a small sacrifice in return for the Great Grace and Magnanimous Mercies You award daily to us. Remind us, Lord, of the power of this simple pitchfork and the beautiful, ordered symmetry that it is able to create in our chaotic lives.

In Your Name Above All names, I humbly pray-

The Power of Three

There is power in the number three
It is easy to recall
Which is reason there are three simple rules
To be considered by one and all.

Finding joy in everything
Widens its circle to many prospects
Praying always and unceasingly
Strengthens us and protects.

Giving thanks whatever the circumstance
Whether it be favorable or adverse
Pleases Our Father who grants us Grace
In ways unpredictable and diverse.

SJ Emmerson

What brought joy today? Did I remember to pray? Was I thankful for all today? What prayers, poems, or ponderings do you have?

17.

Today's Prayer

Fashion Choices

Dear Jesus,

I praise You for this day, a day to clothe ourselves in Your likeness, Instead of choosing to wear anger, malice, rage, slander, lies, or anything related to evil, Your children would more appropriately be clad garments created in by Your Spirit. Words of encouragement, kindness, goodness, humility, joy, and love are much more typically worn by Your children. Lord, help us each and every time we make a decision regarding what to say or how to act to choose the attire that reflects Your Lovingkindness. We always need to be prepared to walk Your red carpet in stylish dignity.

In Your Name Above All names, I humbly pray-

Pretty Clothes

Within each and every hour
Of each and every day
We choose to wear the garments
Stored inside our hearts' cache.

We might choose to don the garments
Made of loving acts of kindness
Or those sewn with hateful, hurtful threads
Damaging and mindless.

Wouldn't it serve a higher plan
To wear words and acts of grace
That encourage and adorn the world
With a smiling, gentler face.

SJ Emmerson

What will my heart wear today? What prayers, poems, or ponderings do you have?

18.

Today's Prayer

The Unlikely Hero

1 Peter 5:5, Matthew 5:5

Dear Jesus,

I praise You for this day, a day to aspire to become an unlikely hero, the one who is both humble and meek. We don't meet many of these in our pride filled, achievement oriented culture. Such characteristics have long been overlooked in favor of self-absorption and occasional egotism. Although the unlikely type of hero has the same capabilities, they aren't ringing their own bells often enough for us to notice the great gifts they give to the world. We don't always hear about the wonderful things they do for others or the almost impossible feats they accomplish. They are the ones, however, who You consider heroes. They do what they do out of authentic love and compassion. They are a lot like you. Lord, help us to be more like You.

In Your Name Above All names, I humbly pray-

The Win

No matter what the odds might be
A victory is ours to gain
On any of life's battlefields
When God is leading our battle's campaign.

Our weapons are not of this world
But rather of Heaven's design
Kindness, forgiveness, humility, love
Are commissioned from The Divine.

We might be just a bit surprised
At the type of victory we receive
But it will be the best sort of win
That we could possibly hope to achieve.

SJ Emmerson

What are my motivations each time I help someone? What prayers, poems, or ponderings do you have?

19.

Today's Prayer

Encouraging Words

1 Thessalonians 5:11, Isaiah 43:2, Romans 15:4

Dear Jesus,

I praise You for today, a day to be thankful for the encouragement we have received from others as well as the opportunities we have been given to return that favor to someone else who needs it. You have given his many Scriptures that can lift us up just when we need it most. You have also placed people, both expected and unexpected, on our paths who have built us up when we needed it the most. Because You have renewed our strength, help us, Lord, to boost someone else up to soar on the wings of eagles, to run and not grow weary. Just as You know everything about each one of us, You know how thirsty we are for a drink of positive support. Thank You for the little dips as well as the extra-large cups of refreshing, delicious encouragement.

In Your Name Above All names, I humbly pray-

Encouragement

A soft, uplifting word or two
Voiced at the perfect time
Can mend a torn and tattered soul
To weave a lovely, new design.

Offering someone a helping hand
Converts a need into a gem
Energizing the weary one
To breathe and start again.

Just being near a grieving heart
Is rain in a desert land
It nourishes the seeds of hope
To grow in the wind tossed sand.

The language of encouragement
Is spoken in many forms
Each and every one of them
Has power to renew and transform.

SJ Emmerson

Who needs encouragement from me today? What are your prayers, poems, and ponderings?

20.

Today's Prayer

The Happy Alternative

Psalm 33:21, Romans 15:13

Dear Jesus,

I praise You for this today, a day to choose joy over all of the grim alternatives that are up for grabs in this world. Your joy is not something contingent to certain circumstances. We should keep an open heart so Your joy can soften the bumps when the road gets rocky. It is one of Your good and perfect gifts sent from above. It would be a regrettable mistake to refuse to receive it under any circumstance. Thank You, Jesus, for the happy gift of joy!

In Your Name Above All names, I humbly pray-

Night and Day

We cannot ever see the stars
If darkness fails to fall
We can't discern the largest heart
Without knowing one that's small.

The heaviness of our burdens
Is far away from sight
Until we've known the warming touch
Of standing in the light.

We don't value or appreciate
An overflowing cup
Unless we've held an empty one
And felt the sting of giving up.

But God has made promise
That the least would be the first
And out of darkness comes the dawn
When His joy will be dispersed.

SJ Emmerson

How can I share God's joy today? What are your prayers, poems, and ponderings?

21.

Today's Prayer

A Pearl of Wisdom

1 Corinthians 16:13-14

Dear Jesus,

I thank You for this day, a day to take heed of St. Paul's pearl of wisdom. We would be wise to be on our guard against evil and stand firm in our faith. Choosing courage and selecting strength are highly recommended options in a world that tries to bend us like a willow twig in a hurricane. The last piece of advice may be the most powerful of all: do everything out of love. That last one is much more powerful than any force of nature. Lord, grant us the wisdom to follow the safe advice written down in Your Book, our best hope for long lasting life.

In Your Name Above All names, I humbly pray-

The Pearl

A little irritation
Caused by a grain of sand
Becomes a pearl within a shell
When touched by Nature's Hand.

The crushing blows of battles lost
Wrought by a hateful foe,
Thrusts open an ironic door of hope
As God makes joy from earthly woe.

When bitter words of others.
Weigh heavy on our minds,
We are only a prayer away
From one whose love always heals and binds.

We need not fear a lasting sting
When stones are aimed and hurled,
Protection comes from a mightier Source,
Christ has overcome the world!

SJ Emmerson

What are your prayers, poems, and ponderings?

22.

Today's Prayer

The Butterflies

2 Samuel 22:33, John 14:67

Dear Jesus,

I praise You for this day, a day to stay on the path You have set before us. Your children are much like the migrating butterflies. They fly in and entertain us with their synchronized aerial dances. Eventually, however, they instinctively follow the path You laid toward their final destination. These mesmerizing creatures possess the same lack of understanding of direction that we experience. They seem to revel in the trees and leaves that are familiar until they are forced by nature to move toward their new home. Lord, keep our feet firmly planted on the paths You would have us take, the ones which will bring us to the home you have been preparing for us. The butterflies will love the mountain forest You have created just for them, and so will we.

In Your Name Above All names, I humbly pray-

The Butterflies Return

Some days are full of problems
With lessons to be learned,
And it feels like a late winter's freeze,
Just before the butterflies return.

Some days bring angry people
To accompany us along our way,
But soft words can turn away such wrath,
And inspire a pleasantly peaceful day.

Some days we must climb mountains
To arrive at a desirable place,
But there's a Mighty One to carry us,
Through the pass and to His Grace.

SJ Emmerson

What "butterflies" did I spot today? What are your prayers, poems, and ponderings?

23.
Today's Prayer

Stained Glass

Matthew 5:16, Psalm 19:14

Dear Jesus,

I praise You for this day, a day to let You Light shine through us like stained glass. When light hits the colors cut from the tinted glass, it pierces through without fading. When we perform heartfelt acts of heartfelt benevolence, Your Light penetrates perfectly through our imperfections and illuminates Your Lovingkindness. Lord, may the words of our mouths, the meditations of our hearts, and our actions shine brightly on You.

In Your Name Above All names, I humbly pray-

The Light

We don't have to sit in darkness
The Light is always there
To lead us to a brighter day
Away from heartache and despair.

We can rise up when we've fallen down
We can always try once more
The Light will lead us on our way
And help us locate different doors.

The dark can shine just like the day
When we look up to Heaven's Light
We just need to keep believing
Even on the blackest nights.

SJ Emmerson

Did I return a gift of turning on a light for someone this week? What prayers, poems, and ponderings do you have?

24.

Today's Prayer

Fully Restored

2 Corinthians 13:11

Dear Jesus,

I praise You for this day, a day to turn to You for full restoration. You restore our hearts, souls, and health. You breathe new life into these human bodies and minds so that we can continue the good works that You have planned for us. Because of Your renewal, we can keep moving forward, and without it we wilt like late August blooms doomed to fade in the heat. Lord, keep us reaching for the Hand that lifts us up to eagles' wings and enables us to see all of the joy surrounding us each day.

In Your Name Above All names, I humbly pray-

The Lion

There's a lion living deep inside
Of every human heart
It roars with strength and fearlessness
Designed to be a fortified rampart.

It stands undaunted in danger's face
Yet tender in peaceful times
A guardian, a protector
Are its ideal paradigms.

Though the lion may be sleeping
When the Peace and Joy draw near
He serves God's purpose boldly
When trouble unexpectedly appears.

SJ Emmerson

How can I adjust my time to get the rest I need? What is making me tired in the first place? What prayers, poems, and ponderings do you have?

25.

Today's Prayer

Reflection

Proverbs 27:19, Isaiah 7:15

Dear Jesus,

I praise You for this day, a day to choose Your Goodness to foster in our hearts. Since our hearts are reflections of who we really are, it would be wise to choose characteristics that are uplifting. If we choose humility over pride, we will extend empathy rather than resentment. Selecting kindness over criticism grows friendship in place of discord. Adopting compassion instead of indifference is essential for building peace. Opting for strength rather than succumbing to weaknesses sets us on a successful course. Settling for self-control rather than over reaction saves us from self-destruction. The choice of thankfulness over fretfulness opens windows for blessings to blow in. Always choosing to love brings us closer to You. Lord, when we fail to make the choices that build Your Kingdom, please replace the tainted ingredients inside our hearts with Your Spirit. There is no more beautiful reflection.

In Your Name Above All names, I humbly pray-

The Poem

Life is a poem, a picture made of words
Sometimes it rhymes, others not so much.
The harmonies can be beautiful
Capable of adding such a special touch.

It is memory, a kaleidoscope
Of both happy times and fallen tears
Tranquil times of peaceful bliss
Days burdened with our frantic fears.

It is a mirror, an exact image
Reflecting the themes of human hearts
It could tell a story that builds us up
Or a tragedy that splits us apart.

Life is a poem, a picture made of words
We are moved by whatever the Author writes
The lines will not keep us in the dark for long
The Author will lead us into the Light.

SJ Emmerson

How can I love better? Who? What are your prayers, poems, and ponderings?

26.

Today's Prayer

His Hand

John 10:28

Dear Jesus,

I praise You for this day, a day to hold tightly to Your Hand and to Your promise of eternal life. We know full-well that this world is filled with evil actions, intentions, and spirits. You, however, will never allow it to snatch us from Your Hand. We may suffer temporary difficulties, but You have overcome the world. Help us, Lord, to count the many blessings we receive along the way and catch us quickly when we inadvertently pull away from Your mighty grip.

In Your Name Above All names, I humbly pray-

Hopeful Hand

Holding on to a Hopeful Hand
Just might open up a door
To a greater Spirit than in the world
Able to refresh, renew, and restore.

Joy is found in the Hand of Hope
There is peace in Its mighty grip
There is no fault in reaching out
The benefits are infinite.

When our world turns gray and cloudy
And the day seems out of control
Seek confidently for the Hopeful Hand
To lift you up and touch your soul.

SJ Emmerson

What do I need to let go and let God? What are your prayers, poems, and ponderings?

27.
Today's Prayer

Quiet Beauty

1 Peter 3:4, Romans 7:22

Dear Jesus,

I praise You for this day, a day to contemplate and nurture the beauty of a gentle and quiet spirit. Such a spirit is very precious to You. Therefore, making room for You to redirect our human inclinations to an angry retort to uncomfortable, unpleasant situations is vital to the practice of gentleness. This quality is so important in Your Kingdom that You consider it a fruit of Your Spirit. Lord, as you know, our pride, our anger, and our hatred sometimes get in the way of a gentle, soft answer. Help us by Your Spirit to overcome these obstacles that block the way to sweet-tempered spirit. Even gentleness in such a harsh environment is possible with You.

In Your Name Above All names, I humbly pray-

Quiet Blessings

When the yawning sun drops away
And stillness is welcomed like a friend.
We can revel in gifts of a different sort
As the quiet blessings greet the day's end.

When we look up at the darkened sky
Or just look up because we must
There are many treasures yet to gain
More subtle and more gently hushed.

With serenity comes a different face
But all faces can host lovely smiles
If we see them through thankful eyes
Quiet blessings are especially worthwhile.

SJ Emmerson

Pride is a problem here, Lord, but I know you are working on it. I need it! What are your prayers, poems, and ponderings?

28.

Today's Prayer

Kept Promises

Psalm 135:13, Deuteronomy 31:8,

Isaiah 40:29, 41:10

Dear Jesus,

I praise You for this day, a day to give thanks for Your kept promises. You are trustworthy in them and faithful in all You do. You strengthen Your children, help us, and uphold us with Your favor! Even at our weakest points, Your Hand provides Power. Riding on these promises is the safest, most comfortable way to travel along the turbulent airways of life. Thank You, Lord, for kept promises. The world may be a fickle friend, but we can truly count on Your steadfast, enduring Love.

In Your Name Above All names, I humbly pray-

Childlike Faith

Out of the mouths of little ones
Words of trust flow freely out
That give them strength against the odds
Negating the fear of menacing doubt.

Jesus welcomed all the children
And proclaimed that they be blessed
With His Kingdom and its treasures
Of greater value than Earth's best.

How much happier we would be
If we practiced the faith of a child
Placing it in the Trusted Source
Perfect and undefiled

SJ Emmerson

What broken promises do I need to "fix"? What are your prayers, poems, and ponderings?

29.
Today's Prayer

The Way

Psalm 16:11, John 3:16

Dear Jesus,

I praise You for this day, a day to be thankful for Your Great Grace that carries us from this life to the next. Because You exchanged Your life for our trip to eternity, we can rest in peace. We have been assured that there is a beautiful new chapter beyond the one we know here on Earth.

You have planned for and created many magnificent opportunities for joy In this life, Lord. Only You and those who have gone before us know about the fullness of that joy we will discover on the other side. Thank You, Jesus, for the comfort of Your Lovingkindness and the promise of our heavenly chapters.

In Your Name Above All names, I humbly pray-

Winter Roses

On frigid, frosty winter days
It is sometimes hard to see
The blooms below the crystal ice
Given out of Grace generously.

We see them when we focus
On the blessings of the storm
On acts of Faithful Lovingkindness
In unexpected, uncommon forms.

Though they do not solve the problems
Blown in by angry winds
They lend to life His beauty
Until the sun returns again.

SJ Emmerson

Why can't I shift my focus a little sooner when I am down?
What are your prayers, poems, and ponderings?

30.

Today's Prayer

Underneath It All

Mark 12: 30-31, Isaiah 26:9, Luke 9:25

Dear Jesus,

I praise You for this day, a day to live from the inside out. You know full well that underneath our flesh and deep within our hearts lives the part of us that travels past our time on this planet. Just as we need to nourish our bodies with good food, we need to nourish our souls with the most sustaining nutrients available. You have richly provided those for us by showing us a love everlasting and also planting the seeds that fall from them-compassion, joy, peace, patience, kindness, goodness, faithfulness, gentleness, and self-control. Help us remember, Lord, to nourish our souls with prayer, thankfulness, praise, and most especially love. Clear away all that is harmful to our souls. Sharpen our vision of You to see Your Lovingkindness in all of the circumstances that envelop us daily. Continue to feed us, Lord, from the inside out.

In Your Name Above All names, I humbly pray

A Work of Art

Sadness often comes with nightfall
It is a hallmark of the dark
A brush with evil forces
An identifying mark.

One gift delivered by the Son of Man
Put limitations on such despair
He exchanges tears for joy
In the morning with loving care.

The Light that rises over darkness
Also illuminates our hearts.
His gladness and his comfort
Paints a joyful work of art.

SJ Emmerson

What behaviors do I practice that do not support the fruits of the Spirit? What are your prayers, poems, and ponderings?

31.

Today's Prayer

The Unexplainable

Ecclesiastes 3:11, Romans 11:13

Dear Jesus,

I praise You for this day, a day to delight in Your creation. You have made everything beautiful in its time. The least we can do is find the time to value the people, the circumstances, the Fingerprints of Your love all around us! You have wrapped us in the beauty of Your steadfast love that endures forever! Although our understanding of it is limited by our humanity, help us, Lord, to see more clearly Your divine strokes in all You have painted into our lives.

In Your Name Above All names, I humbly pray-

Seasonal Selections

Everything is beautiful
In its season and in its time
Like a desert painted by the dawn
Or a transformed caterpillar in its prime.

Everything is beautiful
Even if we do not know
Exactly when the time will come
For beauty to arrive and grief to go.

Everything is beautiful
When it is touched by God's own Hand
We've only to remember
That it is all part of a Greater Plan.

SJ Emmerson

What do I need to add to my prayer life? What prayers, poems, and ponderings do you have?

32.

Today's Prayer

First Family

1 John 3:1

Dear Jesus,

I praise You for this day, a day to ponder the privilege of belonging to Your family. It is, indeed, a great act of Love that You would call us Your children. Our faith alone is enough to be considered one of Your own. As Your children, we are given the keys to an abundant, eternal life with Your Spirit as our guide. Even though we still face Earth's challenges, You will not abandon Your own. Lord, may the words of our mouths, the meditations of our hearts, and our actions all be worthy of our family Name.

In Your Name Above All names, I humbly pray-

The Lasting Gift

There are gifts that can be nice to wear
That enhance appearance and style,
But fashion quickly comes and goes
While kindness is always worthwhile.

Sometimes a gift meets a special need
To help along life's difficult way,
But encouragement that builds the soul
Always brightens the cloudiest days.

Some gifts are inspired by fleeting tastes
And are appealing for a while,
But you can give
Is the gift of a genuine smile.

SJ Emmerson

Am I representing God's family well? How can I improve? What prayers, poems, and ponderings do you have?

33.

Today's Prayer

The Butterflies

2 Samuel 22:33, John 14:67

Dear Jesus,

I praise You for this day, a day to stay on the path You have set before us. Your children are much like the migrating butterflies. They fly in and entertain us with their synchronized aerial dances. Eventually, however, they instinctively follow the path You laid toward their final destination. These mesmerizing creatures possess the same lack of understanding of direction that we experience. They seem to revel in the trees and leaves that are familiar until they are forced by nature to move toward their new home. Lord, keep our feet firmly planted on the paths You would have us take, the ones which will bring us to the home you have been preparing for us. The butterflies will love the mountain forest You have created just for them, and so will we.

In Your Name Above All names, I humbly pray-

When the Butterflies Return

Some days are full of problems
With lessons to be learned,
And it feels like a late winter's freeze,
Just before the butterflies return.

Some days bring angry people
To accompany us along our way,
But soft words can turn away such wrath,
And inspire a pleasantly peaceful day.

Some days we must climb mountains
To arrive at a desirable place,
But there's a Mighty One to carry us,
Through the pass and to His Grace.

SJ Emmerson

What "butterflies" did I spot today? What prayers, poems, and ponderings do you have?

34.

Today's Prayer

Your Light

Matthew 5:16, Psalm 19:14

Dear Jesus,

I praise You for this day, a day to let Your Light shine through us like stained glass. When light hits the colors cut from the tinted glass, it pierces through without fading. When we perform heartfelt acts of heartfelt benevolence, Your Light penetrates perfectly through our imperfections and illuminates Your Lovingkindness. Lord, may the words of our mouths, the meditations of our hearts, and our actions shine brightly on You.

In Your Name Above All names, I humbly pray-

The Light

We don't have to sit in darkness
The Light is always there
To lead us to a brighter day
Away from heartache and despair.

We can rise up when we've fallen down
We can always try once more
The Light will lead us on our way
And help us locate different doors.

The dark can shine just like the day
When we look up to Heaven's Light
We just need to keep believing
Even on the blackest nights.

SJ Emmerson

Did I return a gift of turning on a light for someone this week? What prayers, poems, and ponderings do you have?

35.

Today's Prayer

Reaching to the Heavens

Psalm 57:9-10

Dear Jesus,

I praise You for this day, a day to share with others all of the good things that You have done and continue to do. We live abundantly and forever because Your Love reaches to the heavens. Your faithfulness reaches to the skies. Our souls are safe with You no matter where our feet and our circumstances might take us. Lord, I praise You for the soft, warm blanket You wrap around our hearts in the winter. The cool breeze refreshes our spirits when the summer sun scorches and burns. Your love and faithfulness is never intimidated by the seasonal extremes to which we are exposed.

In Your Name Above All names, I humbly pray-

Prayer for Renewal

For those who need Your shelter
Please hide them with Your wings
May Your Truth be their defense and shield
May they find the comfort Your Presence brings.

For the ones who lie in sickness
Please restore their joy and health
May their faith bring them Healing Power
May Your hope bless their hearts with wealth.

For the lonely and disheartened
Please uphold them through despair
May they find that You are always near
And see the evidence of Your loving care.

For the ones who suffer crippling loss
Please comfort them as they mourn
May they locate new paths cleared for them
May their crushed spirits be reborn.

SJ Emmerson

Where did I see the workings of God's love and faithfulness today? What prayers, poems, and ponderings do you have?

36.

Today's Prayer

Freedom Fighters

Galatians 5:1, Isaiah 41:10, Joshua 1:9

Dear Jesus,

I praise You for this day, a day to be mindful and brimming with thanks for freedom. You set our souls free from the law of sin and death through Your own sacrifices. You even gave us access to Your Spirit. We are free to worship You in ways of our choice because many men and women have given their time, talents, and even lives to ensure this freedom. Lord, help us to reverently remember the people who are currently serving our country as well as those who have given all. Help us to recall daily all that You gave to set us free.

In Your Name Above All names, I humbly pray-

Freely Given

All good and perfect blessings
Come down from Heaven above
Freely given to each one of us
Out of God's compassion, mercy, love.

Because freely we've been given
Freely to others we should give
Cheerfully, willingly, wisely
Purely unselfish alternatives.

As quietly as a mouse we give
God sees the sacrifice arranged
And He rewards most privately
The love inspired gift exchange.

SJ Emmerson

Who do I need to thank for their service? What prayers, poems, or ponderings do you have?

37.

Today's Prayer

The Masterpiece

Ephesians 2:10, Matthew 6:31-3

Dear Jesus,

I praise You for this day to ponder and seek the possibilities You have set into motion for Your children whom You have deemed as masterpieces. You have given us access to all we need to accomplish the goals for which You created us. You turn even our scars into shining stars when we take refuge in You. Our possibilities are as endless as the love You have set aside for each one of us. I praise You for all good plans You have, Lord. Grant us wisdom and guidance to recognize the things You would have us do and strengthen us to move forward with confidence in completing our tasks. Help us to embrace the beauty You have made even from the ashes of our journey and help us to humbly perceive the artistry in every neighbor You place on our paths.

In Your Name Above All names, I humbly pray-

The Masterpiece

God had a Master plan in drawing you
His wonders never cease
Each line, each detail quite unique
Until He formed His masterpiece.

You were born to carry out this plan
The only one who can is you
Perfectly designed for every task
You will ever undertake and pursue.

Just like the greatest of all times
You will surely stand the test
For God's intents, your purposes
You are thoroughly the best.

SJ Emmerson

What are the positive possibilities for me today? What tasks do I need to complete to make them come into fruition? What prayers, poems, and ponderings do you have?

38.

Today's Prayer

The Most Beautiful Story

Psalm 19:1, Isaiah 35:1-2

Dear Jesus,

I praise You for this day, a day to absorb Your beautiful story by observing the colors and various shades of the sunrise and sunset. Today is the time to ponder the deep fuchsia of the four o'clocks growing with abandon in the flower bed. This is a great day to look for evidence of the change of the seasons on the leaves on the trees. It is a day to watch the tiny webfeet creatures born last spring learn to swim on a glass pond surrounded by guardian reeds on the shore. It is a day to catch a twinkle in the eye of a loved one and feel the warmth of their hug. Lord, draw our attention to Your most beautiful story and help us carefully read all of the details, even the parts that are not so pretty. In Your Hand, it is all made beautifully.

In Your Name Above All names, I humbly pray-

His Unchained Melody

I've heard the birds sing in the trees
On bowing branches with bustling leaves
Your lights are seen in August skies
Hopeful twinkles in the dark night's eyes.
The herbal smell of purple sage
When raindrops clean and rearrange.
Silent snow on Saturday
Rich stories shared along life's way.
Smiling, cheerful daffodils,
Bluebonnets covering Texas hills.
Happy fur clad compatriots
Their devotion is warm and salient.
Knowing the touch of little hands
Reaching up to one who understands.
Casual family gatherings
Golden friendships, memories scattering.
A look, a touch, heartfelt support
From the ones who are our first resort.
The crown of children and their own
Lasting love that we have known.
These and countless others play
Your unchained melody every day.

SJ Emmerson

What natural beauty have I observed right around myself today? Did I think to give thanks to God? What prayers, poems, and ponderings do you have?

39.

Today's Prayer

So Much More

Jeremiah 32:27, Matthew 18:26, Luke 1:37

Dear Jesus

I praise You for this day, a day to behold the stream of endless possibilities you have set before us. Nothing is impossible for you, Jesus. The world may deal us unfavorable odds, but You are so much more than this world. We cannot even conceive of just how powerful the mind of the One who set the universes into motion. We cannot imagine how deep or wide the love is of the God who is Love. What we can do is keep searching every day in every way until we meet You face to face. Lord help us to discover Your possibilities in every niche and corner of our lives.

In Your Name Above All Names, I humbly pray-

A Thankful Eye

Thankfulness sweeps away debris
For peace to enter our hearts and minds
It clears the path to positivity
And leaves the negative behind.

Thankfulness is a reminder
That we accomplish little all alone
A grateful heart gives back in part
The kindness that's been shown.

When we view our circumstances
Through the lens of a thankful eye
The good appears even better
And the fearful ceases to terrify.

SJ Emmerson

What possibilities are on my horizon? What prayers, poems, and ponderings do you have today?

40.

Today's Prayer

Soul Streaming

Psalm 46, Psalm 30:11

Dear Jesus,

I praise You for this day. It is a day to be thankful for Your Presence in our lives. Your Spirit, our assurance of Your Presence, is our ever-present help in times of trouble. It is the delightful stream that gives us refuge from the heat of the day and the strength that refreshes and heals our weary souls. With only a drop of its healing water, our wailing is turned to dancing and our sadness into celebration. Its flood of compassion cleanses the sharp stones in our lives and refines them into pure gold.

Please open our ears to hear the rushing water and our eyes to see evidence of the Goodness provided by Your Spirit. Guide us to allow Your Mighty Force to do the work You have planned for us in order to increase the harvest of the Spirit's fruits— love, joy, peace, patience, kindness, goodness, faithfulness, gentleness, and self-control. Against such things there is no law, so help us to remember to feed others from this harvest and not from the harvest of the world.

In Your Name Above All names, I humbly pray-

Evidence

We may never see the Face of God
Or look Him in the Eye
But we can see His sunset's masterpiece
And His palette in the morning's sky.

Christ may not bend to wash our feet
Or turn our water into wine
But we can touch the prints of a baby's hand
And view the perfection of His design.

We may never hear Him call our name
Or listen to angels sing highest praise
But we can feel the Light behind the Word
And sense the Love His Beauty conveys.

SJ Emmerson

What evidence of God have I observed today? What prayers, poems, and ponderings do you have?

41.

Today's Prayer

The Discipline

Psalm 42:5, 31:24, Isaiah 40:31, Jeremiah 29:1

Dear Jesus,

I praise You for this day, a day to practice the discipline of hope. It is not just a passing emotion; hope is a daily practice that we must master in order to find Your Presence on the lead-filled days. In hard times, we can't depend on a mere emotion that disappears like cotton candy in the rain. We must rely on a solid routine of waiting with faith for You to scoop us up, wrap us in Your Loving kindness, and show us the better path to take for our lives. You know the plans You have for us, plans to give us a future and a hope, plans to prosper us and not to harm us. Sharpen our vision with Your Supernatural acuity, Lord, that we might see through what appears to be impenetrable walls of difficulty. We know that what we perceive to be impossible is also as easy as melting cotton candy for You.

In Your Name Above All names, I humbly pray-

The Gift of Hope

Hope is a Hand that lifts our chin
To help us see the morning light
Away from disaster's darkness
A sunnier, buoyant sight.

Hope doesn't have the answers
To our problems small or great
But it lends a tone of harmony
Creating a more positive state.

When our eyes look up instead of down
We aren't as likely to take a fall
Because we can more easily view
The Help that waits for one and all.

SJ Emmerson

What things have given me hope in my life? How can I boost a little hope in someone who needs it? What prayers, poems, and ponderings do you have?

42.

Today's Prayer

On a Lighter Note

John 12:46, Matthew:7:12

Dear Jesus,

I praise You for this day, a day to come into Your Light through Your Word, our prayers, and our worship. You came to illuminate the way for us so that our souls would not be stumbling around in the darkness. You also came so that Your heavenly Light could illuminate our hearts with Your love. We choose to live as children of the Light when we choose to treat others as we would have them treat us. Lord, when we fail to see Your Light, please throw open the shutters of our heart, and let it flood over us once again. May our thoughts, words, and actions bear witness to Your Light.

In Your Name Above All names, I humbly pray-

Children of the Light

In the Light there is no darkness.
It has been shared with everyone
Who believes the Light shines in the dark
Through God's one and only Son.

Those who recognize Its brightness
Know that Love ignites the Light
They need no longer fear death's shadow
Or the obscurity of night.

Those who emit a Loving kindness
That proceeds from deep inside
Most likely belong to the family
Known as the children of the Light.

SJ Emmerson

What darkness do I need to clean up in my thoughts, words, and actions? What prayers, poems, ponderings do you have?

43.

Today's Prayer

New Mercies

Lamentations 3:22-23

Dear Jesus,

I praise You for this day, a day to anticipate Your new mercies that will come our way. They can be disguised as anything--a greeting from a stranger, a lone safety pin in the back of a drawer, toys strewn across a room where a little, but big blessing reminded us of her own mercies. You are our Compassionate Compadre who leaves fresh reminders of His Lovingkindness each and every day. Lord, create in us hearts so clean that we are able to see Your daily blessings whether they are obvious or obscure. I know You enjoy surprising us sometimes. Some of our most memorable mercies are the ones that surprise us the most.

In Your Name Above All names, I humbly pray-

New Everyday

With the rise of morning's light
We receive the gift of dawn.
It comes with mercies undeserved
And forgiveness for selfish wrongs.

God's lovingkindness wakes with us
After seeing us through the night
That we might feast upon His Majesty
In all He created for our delight.

Fresh paths were cleared for us to trod
Carved uniquely for each one.
We are regifted with all necessities
For the journey till day is done.

We've much for which to offer thanks
For the tokens borne of Love
We only need to recognize
That they come first from God Above.

SJ Emmerson

What mercies have I been shown by God? How did I repay such kindness? What are your prayers, poems, and ponderings?

44.

Today's Prayer

Tiny Seeds

Matthew 13:31-32, Zechariah 8:12

Dear Jesus,

I praise You for this day, a day to be thankful for little things. Even the tiniest seeds like the mustard seed can grow up into a beautiful plant. You taught us that our faith is a prime example of this. "Though she is tiny, she is fierce," in the words of Shakespeare. Although the Bard was writing about a woman, our tiniest seeds of faith can also grow into a most impressive garden brimming with purposeful, flowering smiles. Thank You, Lord, for the gift of little things that grow into great joy. Sometimes, they can even move mountains.

In Your Name Above All names, I humbly pray-

Beautiful Seeds

We may not know what grows within
A tiny, helpless seed
But the Master Gardener nurtures it
Until its beauty is complete.

He sends His rain to quench its thirst
And provides soil for nourishment.
His moon grants restful peace of mind
His sun provides encouragement.

The seed unfolds and grows each day
And blooms at its appointed time
To share its beautiful countenance
Planned by the Gardener Sublime.

SJ Emmerson

What seeds did I plant today? How am I nurturing them?
What are your prayers, poems, and ponderings?

45.

Today's Prayer

Spilling Over

John 8:12, 12:36, Psalm 119:130

Dear Jesus,

I praise You for this day. It is a day in which the Light of Your Word spills over into the darkness of the world. The darkness cannot contain it because Light consumes the dark. The Light of day hides only a little while before it reveals itself again and warms the coldness of Earth. Even the night is Light to Your Eyes. Dear Jesus, on cloudy, foggy days, help us to recognize glimmers of Your Light. On bright, sunny days, help us to soak it in and revel in its beauty. At all times, guide us in the ways that we can spread Your Light into the darkness of this world. Thank you, Lord, for spilling over into our lives.

In Your Name Above All names, I humbly pray-

Spilling Over

The sunlight in the morning
Slips over nighttime's veil
Bringing Earth the joyous news
That in Heaven all is well.

A flashlight in the darkness
Engulfs the murkiness of our fears
And lights the way until the rays
Of Daylight's smiling face appears.

The brightest Light we'll ever know
Spills over shadows in our souls
To heal the gloomy brokenness
And free it with a Love that makes it whole.

SJ Emmerson

What are a few of the ways that God has "spilled over" in my life? What are your prayers, poems, and ponderings?

46.

Today's Prayer

The Letter

2 Corinthians 3:2-3

Dear Jesus,

I praise You for this day, a day to ruminate on the letters being written by our lives. Our words are letters to listening ears. Our very lives are letters to those who know us. Please guide us, Lord, by Your Spirit to write the most encouraging words and pen the most loving examples for others to read in the letters written of our lives. You always know exactly what to say.

In Your Name Above All names, I humbly pray-

The Letter

Our words are a letter written
To those who hear us speak
In tones that are harsh and hateful
Or those caring, gentle, meek.

Our lives are a letter written
To those who know us best
With actions that draw others in
Or serve to hurt and to oppress.

Help us, Lord, to choose the words
And actions that speak well of You
Sending messages laced with lovingkindness
Sincerely written, forever true.

SJ Emmerson

What kind of letter did I write today? What are your prayers, poems, and ponderings?

47.
Today's Prayer

Never Alone

Romans 8:35, Psalm 139:7-12

Dear Jesus,

I praise You for this day, a day to rejoice because You are always near to us. You will not totally leave us alone in the darkness of the world. Neither tribulation, distress, persecution, nor any other catastrophe will separate Your Spirit from Your children. Although we do not always sense your presence, You are there to lift us up and carry us either through or away from the situation. Either way it goes, Your Lovingkindness will be as near as our faith in you. Thank You Lord, for following us through all of the ugly places we must travel on Earth. Please don't let us stray away. Love is both our joy and our strength.

In Your Name Above All names, I humbly pray-

The Power of Three

There is power in the number three
It is easy to recall
Which is the reason there are three simple rules
To be considered by one and all.

Finding joy in everything
Widens its circle to many prospects
Praying always and unceasingly
Strengthens us and protects.

Giving thanks whatever the circumstance
Whether it be favorable or adverse
Pleases Our Father who grants us Grace
In ways unpredictable and diverse.

SJ Emmerson

What blessings have I overlooked and said thanks over? What gave me a spark of joy today? Have I prayed and/or petitioned for Big Help? What are your prayers, poems, and ponderings?

48.

Today's Prayer

Listening Ears

Psalm 66:19-20, Lamentations 3:22-24

Dear Jesus,

I praise You for this day, a day to ponder the times You have listened to us. From our hearts to Your ears we pray. You may not always answer our prayers in the way we had hoped, but You always listen. The point to consider on our end is perspective: You see a much wider range of territorial consequences than we see. Sometimes, we may need to pray for better insight into the issue at hand and remember that our heartfelt issues are always in Your Hands. Lord, help us to have at least mustard seed sized faith to see clearly what Your answers really are. Thank You for all answers. Even if the answer is, "No," You still have a good plan for us because Your steadfast Love never ceases; Your mercies never end. As a matter of fact, they are new every morning.

In Your Name Above All names, I humbly pray-

Listening

Listening is the finest art
When done with sincerity
It can reward us with great wisdom,
And plant the seeds of prosperity.

Listening well can help us grow
We learn from those who speak
And when we listen to God Above
We find the Truth we seek.

Listening to the Mighty Voice
Isn't hard; He is everywhere
He talks to us through His Word and world
In whispers of His loving care.

SJ Emmerson

Am I doing more talking than listening to You? How can I listen better? What are your prayers, poems, and ponderings?

49.

Today's Prayer

The Oaks

Isaiah 61:3-4, Jeremiah 17:18, 39:18

Dear Jesus,

I praise You for this day, a day to cling tightly to our trust in You. When we put our faithful hope in Your unfailing Love, we grow strong like ancient oak trees whose leaves are evergreen. They stand securely through violent storms. Their hardy roots tunnel deep into the earth to drink in spite of drought. Acorns fall from their branches to cover the ground, ensuring their continuance. Lord, remind us to plant ourselves in You so that we can stand strong, refreshed, and renewed throughout our days.

In Your Name Above All names, I humbly pray-

The Live Oak

Planted by the river
The live oak strives and thrives
As it digs deep within the soil
For water to survive.

Storms strike the tree with mighty winds
To bend and break a limb
But Nature's strength and perseverance
Delivers much needed inspiration.

Seasons wrapped in years pass by
Birds nest before their flight
Its acorns fall and plant new hope
For the oak to reach new heights.

SJ Emmerson

Which areas of myself need toughening? What are your prayers, poems, and ponderings?

50.

Today's Prayer

Serious Conversations

Ephesians 6:18, 1:16-18

Dear Jesus,

I praise You for this day, a day to come into Your Presence through our heart-felt prayers. The privilege of a personal relationship with You is extraordinary to say the very least. You are not only a God who sees us, but You are a God who also listens. When we come to You and call on You, You are always there to hear us. Like a Good Shepherd, You know our needs before we ask, but our acts of faithful prayer remind us to pray in our hearts, Lord, at all times and in all circumstances. Your kingdom, power, and glory are the ones that last forever.

In Your Name Above All names, I humbly pray-

The Lifeline

When you dive into deep, dark water
And your air is running low
Look up and tug your Lifeline
To lift you from below.

If you're climbing up the mountainside
And your foot begins to slip
Hold on tight to that Lifeline
To avoid a fatal trip.

No matter where your journey leads
Be it the heights or depths of life
God's Lifeline is offered free to you
To ensure that you will survive.

SJ Emmerson

What have I taken to the Lifeline today? What are your prayers, poems, and ponderings?

51.

Today's Prayer

Running the Race

2 Timothy 4:7-8, Matthew 19:26

Dear Jesus,

I praise You for this day, a day to run hard the race set before us. We already know it will be difficult, but with Your help, all things are possible. Through our faith in Your unfailing Love, we find strength and help when we most need it. You lift us up on eagle's wings when we most need it and carry us when we can no longer run. Lord, grant us the strength and stamina to successfully run the races You set forth for us to run. Keep our eyes focused on You for direction. We can't even imagine how wonderful Your prize will be when we reach the finish line.

In Your Name Above All names, I humbly pray-

One Small Step

One small step at a time
That is all we have to do
One kind word to a needy ear
Before the day is through.

A random act of kindness
To someone we may not know
Could turn someone's day around
When they are feeling low.

Just a smile freely given
Asking nothing in return
Might spark a chain reaction
Erasing the most stressful of concerns.

A short moment or two shared
With a sad and lonely heart
Can be such a happy time
For a world completely torn apart.

Loving our neighbors as ourself
Is not a complicated command.
God's love shines in the small mercies
Just the same as in the grand.

SJ Emmerson

What areas are too weak to finish the races that have come across my path? What are your prayers, poems, and ponderings?

52.

Today's Prayer

Sure-footed

Psalm 37:23-24, Jude 24

Dear Jesus,

I praise You for this day, a day to walk joyfully into the thick of it because You are directing our steps. We will likely stumble from time to time, but You will be there to catch us. You hold tightly to our hands as we move through each day keeping us upright and moving gingerly toward a heavenly goal. Thank You, Lord, for directing our steps to unimaginable and beautiful destinations. Although the roads are sometimes bumpy, You never fail to pick us up, dust us off, and keep us moving ahead. Thank You for the Divine roadside assistance You provide. We would be lost without it.

In Your Name Above All names, I humbly pray-

All Is Bright

The fabric of our world is torn
By wars and spiteful crimes
Envy and hate stirring the atmosphere
Keep life far away from the sublime.

Heaven's story sets a different tone
Where darkness bows to Light
Peace and joy are everywhere
All is calm, and all is bright.

I wonder how the world would change
If we focused on Love and Light
Would there be a different atmosphere?
Would all be calm; would all be bright?

SJ Emmerson

What are some examples of God re-routing my footsteps?
What are your prayers, poems, and ponderings?

53.

Today's Prayer

Lost and Found

Luke 1:1-10

Dear Jesus,

I praise You for this day, a day to take comfort in the fact that there is always Someone who will find us when we are lost. There is much joy in heaven over finding one who has strayed off course and finds himself in the middle of nowhere. Lord, when we wander into unknown territory, please remind us to look up for Your guidance. I know You will be waiting to pick us up, dust us off, and carry us back home for the celebration that awaits us.

In Your Name Above All names, I humbly pray-

Children of the Light

In the Light there is no darkness.
It has been shared with everyone
Who believes the Light shines in the dark
Through God's one and only Son.

Those who recognize Its brightness
Know that Love ignites the Light
They need no longer fear death's shadow
Or the obscurity of night.

Those who emit a Loving kindness
That proceeds from deep inside
Most likely belong to the family
Known as the children of the Light.

SJ Emmerson

Are there pieces of my life that need to be dusted off and filled with Your light? What prayers, poems, and ponderings do you have?

54.
Today's Prayer
Tough Love
Luke 6:38, 1 John 2:10

Dear Jesus,

I praise You for this day, a day to give of ourselves to others out of love. It is written that the measure with which we give is the measure we receive. Sometimes, we would rather choose to fight with others, but making the choice to generously give of ourselves to those who wish us ill is the way to peace. I truly believe that everything we are asked to do is asked from the standpoint of pure love you have for Your children. Help us, Lord, to spread Your Light as well as illuminate our own world. Your ideas are always the best and brightest ones.

In Your Name Above All names, I humbly pray-

The Decision

Love is a decision
The wisest ever made
Because it is the heart of God
His Spirit on Earth portrayed.

Love is a decision
The kindest one to share
It lifts up others near and far
To let them know we care.

Love is a decision
To leave the world a better place
With a peaceful atmosphere
Of happiness and great grace.

SJ Emmerson

Make a list of the times God has loved me through times when I did not deserve it. Who do I need to forgive? What are your ponderings, poems, and ponderings?

55.

Today's Prayer

The Fortress

Psalm 59:16-17, 5:11

Dear Jesus,

I praise You for this day, a day to be thankful for Your fortress of protection when we need to escape from the enemies that attack us in this world. Your stronghold is fortified with the most powerful weapon-- Lovingkindness. You, Lord, laid down Your life for Your believers and were raised again to sit beside our Father in Heaven. With You to protect us, we can conquer the evil that surrounds us and win our battles over worldly woe. Strengthen us, God of the Possible. Nothing is impossible to You.

In Your Name Above All names, I humbly pray-

The Fortress

Faith is believing in what we can't see
Like His Word that is good and true.
No feat will be impossible
If we keep our trust in You.

Please help us hold tight to our faith
Even when things fall apart.
You will be there on the worst of days
To protect us and to stand guard.

SJ Emmerson

What examples of miracles have I witnessed? What are your prayers, poems, or ponderings?

56.

Today's Prayer

The Scattering of Light

Hebrews 1:3

Dear Jesus,

I praise You for this day, a pause and soak up Your radiance. Your Word scatters the Light of Our Father, God of Love. In Your Light is all power and glory. Healing rays touch our hearts and minds. Rest comes easy in Your Presence because there is nothing to fear. You enable us to do the unimaginable as the One through whom all was created. Lord, there is no logical reason not to enter into Your Light as often as we can. Please guide us to select an automatic scheduling of catching Your rays of love and light.

In Your Name Above All names, I humbly pray-

In the Stillness

In the stillness of the morning,
In the quiet of early day,
I can feel His Spirit nudging me
To close my eyes and pray.

In the stillness of the morning,
In the quiet of early day,
His Word is waiting patiently
For me to study without delay.

In the stillness of the morning,
In the quiet of early day,
I will praise Him for His boundless love
He shares richly along life's way.

SJ Emmerson

Did I get still enough to catch some of the rays of Heaven coming my way today? What were those blessings? What are your prayers, poems, and ponderings?

57.

Today's Prayer

Joyful, Patient, Faithful

Dear Jesus,

I praise You for this day, a day to be joyful in hope, patient in affliction, and faithful in prayer. Even if things don't go our way today, we can always be hopeful because of You. You have the ability to turn our scars into stars on a dime! We have only to be patient and wait for You to move. Even if we don't perceive such a transformation, we can always rest assured of Your steadfast Love which is so great that we cannot even fathom the height, depth or width of it. Prayers are one of our best communication devices to tap into Your peace and hopeful joy. Keep our minds and hearts set on You and Your Great Grace. You ask little of us considering we receive eternal, abundant life in return.

In Your Name Above All names, I humbly pray-

Evergreen

In the back of the forest
Stands the mighty evergreen
Silent protector and provider
Of creatures visible and those unseen.

It shelters friends and foes alike
Its love knows no limits or bounds
It helps all creatures who come near
So their lives may thrive and abound.

Just like that splendid, noble tree
Is Heaven's perfect Evergreen
Sharing His blessings of abundant life
From Hands that reign supreme.

SJ Emmerson

What scars of mine have been transformed into stars? What are your prayers, poems, and ponderings?

58.

Today's Prayer

Listening Ears

Psalm 66:19-20

Dear Jesus,

I praise You for this day, a day to ponder the times You have listened to us. From our hearts to Your ears we pray. You may not always answer our prayers in the way we had hoped, but You always listen. The point to consider on our end is perspective: You see a much wider range of territorial consequences than we see. Sometimes, we may need to pray for better insight into the issue at hand and remember that our heartfelt issues are always in Your Hands. Lord, help us to at least have mustard seed sized faith to see clearly what Your answers really are. Thank You for all answers. Even if the answer is, "No," You still have a good plan for us because Your steadfast Love never ceases; Your mercies never end. As a matter of fact, they are new every morning.

In Your Name Above All names, I humbly pray-

The Finest Art

Listening is the finest art
When done with sincerity
It can reward us with great wisdom,
And plant the seeds of prosperity.

Listening well can help us grow
We learn from those who speak
And when we listen to God Above
We find the Truth we seek.

Listening to the Mighty Voice
Isn't hard; He is everywhere
He talks to us through His Word and world
In whispers of loving care.

SJ Emmerson

Am I doing more talking than listening to You? How can I listen better? What are your prayers, poems, and ponderings?

59.

Today's Prayer

Great Advice

Philippians 4:6

Dear Jesus,

I praise You for this day, a day to pray in all situations. It is a day to send up our petitions along with our thanksgiving to the One who listens intently and intercedes for us. Guide our hearts and minds often into prayer, Lord. When we do this, Your peace which passes all understanding will guard our hearts and minds.

In Your Name Above All names, I humbly pray-

Just Pray

For those who need Your shelter
Please hide them with Your wings
May Your Truth be their defense and shield
May they find the comfort Your Presence brings.

For the ones who lie in sickness
Please restore their joy and health
May their faith bring them Healing Power
May Your hope bless their hearts with wealth.

For the lonely and disheartened
Please uphold them through despair
May they find that You are always near
May they see evidence of Your loving care.

For the ones who suffer crippling loss
Please comfort them as they mourn
May they locate new paths cleared for them
May their crushed spirits be reborn.

SJ Emmerson

I know I have overlooked the option of praying many times. What are some situations I have neglected in prayer? What prayers, poems, and ponderings do you have?

60.

Today's Prayer

Fixed

Psalm 16:8-11, John 10:10

Dear Jesus,

I praise You for this day, a day to keep our eyes fixed on You so that we will not be shaken from our faith. We are free to know life's eternal and abundant pleasures because You are there selflessly interceding for us. We are safe on Your relentless watch. Lord, the joy we know in Your Presence is our strength. Help us keep our eyes fixed on it, especially in the dark when we begin to stumble around.

In Your Name Above All names, I humbly pray-

Fixed

When our eyes are fixed on the sunshine
We cannot see the dark.
The sunny rays spill over
Surrounding us with their sparks.

When we ponder things like noble deeds
Things lovely, true, or pure
Admirable or worthy of praise
Our minds are peaceful and reassured.

These things are gifts from Heaven
Coming down from God Above
Tools to use to solve our problems
Not tools of war, but tools of Love.

SJ Emmerson

How much of my day was spent on fixing my eyes on you?
What are your prayers, poems, and ponderings?

61.

Today's Prayer

Lifted and Exalted

Isaiah 52:13, Philippians 2:9-11

Dear Jesus,

I praise You for this day, a day to commemorate the One who was both lifted up and exalted. Your coming was foretold centuries before Your arrival, but all that time You were preparing the way for us to accept You into our hearts. Knowing that You would be lifted up on a cross before You were lifted back up into Heaven, You still came to give us a real and lasting life. Lord, there really is no thanks strong enough except to give our hearts to the One who gave us everything.

In Your Name Above All names, I humbly pray-

Prayer for Hope

Dear God,
Thank You for Your promises
That fill our lives with hope
They lift our spirits when they sink
And keep our hearts afloat.

Please hold us close and keep us safe
Through the day and all night long
Fix our minds on hopeful thoughts
That make us confident and strong.

SJ Emmerson

What am I holding back from serving others? What are your prayers, poems, and ponderings?

62.

Today's Prayer

Full

Psalm 107:9, Romans 12:2

Dear Jesus,

I praise You this day for all of the goodness with which You fill our hearts and minds. We will never be hungry for love, joy, peace, and all of their soul-satisfying nutrients. When we seek You out and ask, You will supply the truest longings of our hearts and minds. Lord, thank You for quenching the thirst and hunger of our hearts, and thank You for all answered prayers. Guide us to be generous in sharing much needed provisions to other hearts.

In Your Name Above All names, I humbly pray-

The Rising Sun

Hope rides high with the rising sun,
As we start a newborn day,
Untouched opportunities arise
When the old have gone their way.

Joy escorts the dawning day,
We need only let it be,
It rewards the soul with glad delight
And relieves the heart's poverty.

New life is born with morning's Light,
When it fills night's darkest void,
Its endless benefit to a finite world
Is its inability to ever be destroyed.

SJ Emmerson

How can I bring Light into a dark place? What are your prayers, poems, and ponderings?

63.

Today's Prayer

Numbering Our Days

Psalm 90:12

Dear Jesus,

I praise You this day, a day to celebrate You in every moment because the days of our lives here on this planet are numbered. In order to complete all of the plans You have for us, we must manage our time and resources wisely and make the most out of both the common and the extraordinary moments You have built into our earthly experiences. All things are beautiful and purposeful in their season. Help us, Lord, to celebrate You in all that we think, say, and do. Guide us to make our moments count in Your Kingdom.

In Your Name Above All names, I humbly pray-

Home

Smiling face inside the door
The touch of a familiar hand
An ear that listens attentively
A mind that understands.

Early quiet coffee time
Watching February's icy snow
Observing Spring's first petals form
Crooning birds flying to and fro.

A precious princess perfect pup
Trips to see her special friends
Lighthearted laughter, story spells
Extraordinary moments to apprehend.

The simple things are treasure troves
Because they're shared with you
Loving care weaves a safety net
Where hearts can rest and be renewed.

SJ Emmerson

How and who can I comfort today? What are your prayers, poems, and ponderings?

64.

Today's Prayer

Together

Ecclesiastes 4:9-10, 1 Peter 4:8-10

Dear Jesus,

I praise you for this day, a day to be thankful for our friends and a day to be the friends You would have us to be. A gathering of two or more is a powerful force. They can be strong for each other. When we gather in Your name You have promised to join us. Friends and family are among Your most treasured gifts. Having someone travel alongside us makes the good times so much better and lessons the bumps and bruises of the rocky times. Lord, help us to remember to extend our hospitality wholeheartedly to others. Remind us of the ways we can use our gifts to serve others in all the ways you planned for each one of us. Above all, help us to love. It covers most of our blemishes.

In Your Name Above All names, I humbly pray-

Reflection on Friendship

Friends laugh with you when you are happy,
And cushion your heart when you fall,
They listen to your whispers,
And celebrate your moments both great and small.

Friends easily predict your behavior,
They know your silent thoughts,
They feel your needs unspoken,
And offer to help before it is sought.

Friends encourage the best that is in you,
They uncover those special gifts.
When you forget your own uniqueness,
They can give your soul a lift.

Friends can give you honesty's treasure,
Even when the words may sting,
But when spoken for your greater good,
This gift imparts a tender understanding.

In this life wealth may be fleeting,
And fame vanishes in the wind.
God can work through those nearest us,
You are rich if you have a friend.

SJ Emmerson

When and how do I gather and pray with others? What are your prayers, poems, and ponderings?

65.

Today's Prayer

Closer Than a Brother

Proverbs 17:17, Colossians 3:12

Dear Jesus,

I praise You for this day, a day to be thankful for our friends. They are Your Hand on us in good times and in bad. When one falls down, the other is there to help the fallen one. Our friends bear our failures, believe in us when it doesn't make sense to do so, always hope for the best in us, and they endure the darkest days with us. Their love for us is a mirror of Your love. Our friends are special gifts that are borne from the Light of Your Love. Lord, show us how we can best demonstrate compassion, kindness, humility, gentleness, and patience to our friends. They surely shed a great deal of Your Light into our lives.

In Your Name Above All names, I humbly pray-

A Beautiful Soul

A beautiful soul is a sight to behold
A ray of sunshine on a rainy day
A sharing, caring wondrous work
A paragon in friendship's bouquet.

Wearing garments of rich compassion
Accessories made of generosity's jewels
Serving guests with warm hospitality
And a gift of a heart's renewal.

A wise decision it is, indeed,
To befriend such a beautiful soul
A safe haven in a danger zone
A home both to share joys or be consoled.

SJ Emmerson

Which of the fruits of the Spirit do I most often share? When have I shared each one of them with a friend or neighbor? What are your prayers, poems, and ponderings?

66.

Today's Prayer

The Best Medicine

Luke 6:21, Proverbs 17:22

Dear Jesus,

I praise You for this day, a day to swallow Your best medicine—laughter. There are absolutely times when we weep for valid reasons here on Earth, but when those times pass, we must take every opportunity to laugh and be joyful. Such a treatment is unadulterated, pure, and organic. There are no harmful side effects to a good laugh. The only side effect is the smile that accompanies the chuckles. Lord, along with the chemicals prescribed by our doctors, help us to remember to swallow a little laughter today. We all need a spoonful or two each day.

In Your Name Above All names, I humbly pray-

The Best Medicine

All human capabilities
Are important in order to survive
But the highly underrated one
Adds enormous quality to our lives.

Laughter is like medicine
For the outlook and the mind.
It is vital to one's attitude,
Restores the spirit and helps the body to rewind.

It is of priceless value
As a holistic, healing force
There is no negative side-effect
Free to whomever swallows it,
A prized medicinal resource.

SJ Emmerson

What did I laugh about today? How have I helped a friend today? What are the gifts I can use to encourage friends? What are your prayers, poems, and ponderings?

67.

Today's Prayer

Holding Fast

Romans 12:19, 1 John 4:1

Dear Jesus,

I praise You for this day, a day to hold fast to all that is good and let go of anything that is not. You have instructed us to be wise, to test what is good. We need Your wisdom, Lord, to do this as there is much trickery and deceit out in the world. You warned us of it. Lord, grant us wisdom to discern what is wise. Tighten our grip on everything good. Bathe our hearts in sincere love for You and for others.

In Your name Above All names, I humbly pray-

The Discovery

Each day is a new adventure
For seeing evil or finding good
But the one that leads to happiness
Is sometimes misunderstood.

God's fingerprints are found on both
If we take a careful, faith-filled look.
His Hand can change the dark to light
By His finger's slightest crook.

Perhaps the grandest discovery
Throughout the adventure of our days
Is not only locating the beauty
But seeing it in the harm that stands in our way.

SJ Emmerson

To what am I clinging? Is it good or bad? What are your prayers, poems, and ponderings?

68.
Today's Prayer

Way Maker

Psalm 16:11, Acts 2:28

Dear Jesus,

I praise You for this day, a day to choose joy as we walk down paths laid out for us. The way You have made known to us is the way to truth and life. It is a life full of loving you in heart, mind, and soul. It is also the path to treat our neighbors as we would have them treat us out of a heart that loves unconditionally. It is a life of using our gifts and talents to achieve these goals. It isn't always easy, but it is the one which leads us to the very best places. Lord, keep us traveling along on Your paths that lead to Your heavenly Love and Light. Help discover every glimmer of joy along the way.

In Your Name Above All names, I humbly pray-

The Game

The game of life is a tricky one
Much harder than we expect
No matter how well we plan
The path is bumpy and indirect.

We sometimes feel inadequate
And other times total defeat
But we must always remember
It's not over until the game is complete.

So if you find you're way behind
And in a downward spin
Look Up then play your best life's game
And you will surely take home the win.

SJ Emmerson

How am I making myself accountable for staying on Your path? What are your prayers, poems, and ponderings?

69.

Today's Prayer

Declarations of Appreciation

Psalm 119:62, 42:8

Dear Jesus,

I praise You for this day, a day to declare our thankfulness for all of the acts of grace, mercy, and lovingkindness You have rendered to us. Throughout our days and nights, You have done great things for us. We are still here and headed for eternity because of the seen and unseen acts of true love and devotion You lavish on us. Lord, from sunrise to sunrise make us mindful of the blessings given from Your ever-flowing fountain of Lovingkindness. Write them on our hearts and remind us to speak of them often.

In Your Name Above All names, I humbly pray-

A Thankful Eye

Thankfulness sweeps away debris
For peace to enter our hearts and minds
It clears the path to positivity
And leaves the negative behind.

Thankfulness is a reminder
That we accomplish little all alone
A grateful heart gives back in part
The kindness that's been shown.

When we view our circumstances
Through the lens of a thankful eye
The good appears even better
And the fearful ceases to horrify.

SJ Emmerson

How can I make thanksgiving a part of my daily routine? What am I thankful for today? What are your prayers, poems, and ponderings?

70.

Today's Prayer

Fullness of Grace

John 1:16, 2 Corinthians 9:8

Dear Jesus,

I praise You for this day, a day to ponder the fullness of His grace. If we look up, we see slices of an infinite sky filled with more wonders uncovered than we can ever discover. If we look across the land, the variety of ecosystems, flora, and fauna feed and nourish all of our senses. Below the earth and throughout the oceans we are graced with abundant life that intrigues us and sustains the earth. Our loved ones and relationships are touches of His Great Grace that feed our hearts and lives. His Word and our life altering opportunity to experience Your Spirit and open our hearts to Your Kingdom of love and light are more valuable than anything we can imagine. Lord, help us to cherish the gifts of Your Great Grace we have been given. Even when we don't understand the meaning behind the gift, we are still graced with Your Presence. You always make a way for Your Grace to find us.

In Your Name Above All names, I humbly pray-

Evening on River Road

A water-color melting sun
Sinks into a mirror-covered lake.
Honeysuckle and jasmine friends
Meet once more to celebrate.

The cardinals and the finches feed
Squirrels scurry from tree to tree
Provided by a generous hand
And given away for free.

The geese on river's island pause
For rest after a day's worth of play.
Stealthily, cotton candy clouds
Slip in for a long night's stay.

A peaceful night awaits the dawn
If man will only let it be.
Then rest and renewal can enter in
To leave their life-giving legacy.

SJ Emmerson

What are some of the unexpected ways God has shown me His Grace? What are your prayers, poems, and ponderings?

71.

Today's Prayer

Be Still

Mark 4:39-41, Psalm 107:29, Hebrews 1:3

Dear Jesus,

I praise You for this day, a day to listen to Your calming words and trust that You have everything under control. You calmed the raging sea for Your disciples, for Moses, and for Jonah. You can surely calm me. You are the exact representation of Our Father. With Your Word, You uphold all things. Lord, when the waves are looming high over me, help me to remember that You have the proven ability to calm both the sea and to calm me.

In Your Name Above All names, I humbly pray-

God's Eyes

God's eyes see passed the obvious
Seeing deep within our hearts.
His view spans every moment lived
With all life's stops and starts.

They gaze on us with tenderness
From a Father's point of view.
Though He knows our thoughts and motives
He still loves us through and through.

We can't hide from such keen vision
It is foolish to even try
But we can always seek His guidance
And stand willing to comply.

SJ Emmerson

What deep water experiences can I recall? How did God still my storm? What prayers, poems, and ponderings do you have?

72.

Today's Prayer

The Overseer

Philippians 1:6, Psalm 138:8

Dear Jesus,

I praise You for this day, a day to move confidently through the projects that we have begun. Wherever we are in the process, You will see us through to the completion of our tasks. You put each one of them into motion, and You make certain that our missions are accomplished successfully by Your standards which may or may not be our own. We are the work of Your Hands, the children of the great Creator who were awarded gifts and talents with which to create joy and goodwill for our neighbors. Lord, please perfect the work of Your children. Make a way for our creations to build Your Kingdom of love and light. We are the work of Your Hands.

In Your Name Above All name, I humbly pray-

The Dove

God promises His peace of mind
To those who trust in Him
He offers daily mercies
And seeks to save rather than to condemn.

His peace cannot be bought or sold
We find it in His Word
In prayer and in quiet times
When in our hearts His Voice is heard.

He sent His Son, The Prince of Peace
To demonstrate His Love
With an offer to exchange our fears
For the peace of Heaven Above.

SJ Emmerson

What projects do I have to finish? Have I given them to my Boss to implement? What prayers, poems, and ponderings do you have?

73.

Today's Prayer

Practice Meets Perfect

1 Corinthians 9:24, Hebrews 12:2

Dear Jesus,

I praise You for this day, a day to keep practicing the art of becoming like You. First, we must fix our eyes on You, the author and Perfector of our faith. We must also immerse ourselves in Your Word so we can see through Your example of behavior. Finally, we must repeat the behavior over and over. Great athletes do this. Great chefs, painters, writers, professionals all do this. In fact, the masters of any art or craft do this. The more we repeat something in thought, word, or deed, the more we become what we do. Your followers knew this long before the cognitive behavioral therapists did. Lord, help us keep our eyes fixed on You. Be near us as we practice Your example until we can see You face-to-face.

In Your Name Above All names, I humbly pray-

Seeds

Although its seed is very small
With encouragement hope will grow.
The flowers grown from one tiny pod
Bloom into a magnificent show.

Worthwhile it is to plant such seeds
Their harvest breeds happy souls
Filled with confidence and dignity
To accomplish inspired goals.

The roots of hope reach far and wide
Spreading across the human heart
Cultivating God's great peace and love
That make life an eternal work of art.

SJ Emmerson

What behaviors need more practice in my own life? What are your prayers, poems, and ponderings?

74.

Today's Prayer

Calming the Waves

Mark 4:38-39, Psalm 107:29

Dear Jesus,

I praise You for this day, a day to place our faith in Your uncanny ability to calm the waves that sweep up over our lives. With two little words "Be still," the waves covering Your disciples' boat retreated, and the angry sea relaxed again. It is so with the upheaval we experience in our lives as well. Our waves come and go, sometimes they seem to be tsunami size, but Your words are more powerful than nature itself. Why wouldn't it be? You were right there overseeing the construction of it all. Lord, when the boats get tossed and life's vicious waves cover us, help us to hear Your voice calming them. It is our lullaby and our peace.

In Your Name Above All names, I humbly pray-

Rainbow's Promise

The rainbow spreads across the sky
After the storm ceases all its play
Promising a sunnier circumstance
Coming a bit later in the day.

Butterflies float upon the breeze
Demonstrating colorful grace
Displaying beauty in transformation
With an unexpectedly lovely face.

The lark sings songs in early morn
When darkness slyly slips away
Heralding hope for new life and for Light
And answers to prayers we have prayed.

SJ Emmerson

Why is it that I sometimes choose panic in bad times over asking God for help? What are your prayers, poems, and ponderings?

75.

Today's Prayer

Cleaning Day

Psalm 51:10, 2 Corinthians 5:17

Dear Jesus,

I praise You for this day. It is a cleaning day for our hearts and minds. We are Your new creations, the old has passed away. Our spirits are at their best when they are clean and pure. The jealousies, resentment, and hate. should be thrown away and replaced. Instead of constantly wanting the latest and greatest "toys", we should focus on contentment and thanksgiving. Humility is worthy of reward, not pride, so we need to react in humility when we are tempted to boast. Instead of jealousy and envy, we should be happy for our neighbors when fortune comes their way. Grace is a far more constructive response than resentment, and love always wins over hatred. Our thoughts and words should encourage others as well as ourselves. Our social and private consumption should bring us peace of mind, not confusion. sadness, or depression. Lord, strengthen us to allow Your Spirit to clean the unreachable sections of our hearts and minds so that Your love, joy, peace, patience, kindness, goodness, faithfulness, gentleness, and self-control can settle into every part of us. You are where our deepest happiness is found.

In Your Name Above All names, I humbly pray-

Cleaning Up

Sweep away the sadness
So joy can rule your day
The sky will be much bluer
When you sweep the clouds away.

Wash away resentments
If they leave a dirty smudge
Leave behind resentful thoughts
They tend to stir up a grudge.

Mop up all the jealousy
That trips up our happiness
Spread light and love wherever you go
And open your heart to a grace-filled focus.

SJ Emmerson

What do I need to clean up in my heart and how can I do it?
What are your prayers, poems, and ponderings?

76.

Today's Prayer

Calming the Waves

Mark 4:38-39, Psalm 107:29

Dear Jesus,

I praise You for this day, a day to place our faith in Your uncanny ability to calm the waves that sweep up over our lives. With two little words "Be still," the waves covering Your disciples' boat retreated, and the angry sea relaxed again. It is so with the upheaval we experience in our lives as well. Our waves come and go, sometimes they seem to be tsunami size, but Your words are more powerful than nature itself. Why wouldn't it be? You were right there overseeing the construction of it all. Lord, when our boats get tossed and life's vicious waves cover us, help us to hear Your voice calming them. It is our lullaby and our peace.

In Your Name Above All names, I humbly pray-

The Only Battle

The only battle worth waging
Is the battle to make lasting peace.
Everyone wins when the conflict,
And the arguments finally cease.

No one is destroyed in such a battle
Because all dignity is preserved.
No one's feelings are wounded,
Everyone gets the respect they deserve.

The warriors can lay down their weapons.
Their weary souls and hearts can find rest.
When the battle for peace is finally won
We free ourselves to be happily blessed.

SJ Emmerson

What are some of the hard times when I needed to rely on Jesus? What are your prayers, poems, and ponderings?

77.

Today's Prayer

Night and Day

John 10:10, 1 Peter 5:8, Psalm 23

Dear Jesus,

I praise You for this day, a day to choose to live in the light rather than flounder around in the darkness. The spirit of night is a thief standing ready to snatch us away like sheep from the goodness of the Shepherd. Your Spirit watches over us like a Good Shepherd that seeks to preserve and maximize the life of His flock. Lord, as You well know, we need heavy security to guard us throughout the dark night. Spiritual thieves run rampant in such times. Thank You for the abundance of life giving protection and the sunshine of Your Lovingkindness shared with us.

In Your Name Above All names, I humbly pray-

Night and Day

We cannot ever see the stars
If darkness fails to fall
We can't discern the largest heart
Without knowing one that's small.

The heaviness of our burdens
Is far away from sight
Until we've known the warming touch
Of standing in the light.

We don't value or appreciate
An overflowing cup
Unless we've held an empty one
And felt the sting of giving up.

But God has made promise
That the least would be the first
And out of darkness comes the dawn
When His joy will be dispersed.

SJ Emmerson

What choices do I make that help myself find the light? What prayers, poems, and ponderings do you have?

78.

Today's Prayer

No Eye

1 Corinthians 2:9-10, Job 5:9-10

Dear Jesus,

I praise You for this day. This is the day to be grateful for the unimaginable scope of all You have freely given to us. It is too much for our eyes to see, our ears to hear, and our hearts to absorb at one time. Your wonders cannot be fathomed, nor Your miracles counted. Little by little, we glance at the magnanimous nature of You and Our Father. You, indeed, have given Your children much for which to anticipate. Lord, please guide us in returning goodness to those You have placed in our paths. Help us to love more authentically and serve others more efficiently. May Your praise be always on our lips.

In Your Name Above All names, I humbly pray-

Rainbow's Promise

The rainbow spreads across the sky
After the storm ceases all its play
Promising a sunnier circumstance
Coming a bit later in the day.

Butterflies float upon the breeze
Demonstrating colorful grace
Displaying beauty in transformation
With an unexpectedly lovely face.

The lark sings songs in early morn
When darkness slyly slips away
Heralding hope for new life and for Light
And answers to prayers we have prayed.

SJ Emmerson

What miracles do I witness daily? What prayers, poems, and ponderings do you have?

79.

Today's Prayer

In Service

1 Peter 4:10

Dear Jesus,

I praise You for this day, a day to use our gifts wisely in service to others. Our gifts are not meant to be hoarded, but rather to be shared. Just as Your Great Grace comes in many forms, we each have a unique purpose to fulfill as Your children. Our gifts are the tools we have received to build Your Kingdom of Lovingkindness in the hostile environment of Earth. They are not meant for self-promotion, but rather for selfless giving. Lord, when we are tempted to pride ourselves in our gifts, remind us that they are intended to be used humbly. Help us to follow Your example of giving love offerings to Our Father and our neighbors. People may not remember what we gave to them, but they will always remember how we made them feel.

In Your Name Above All names, I humbly pray-

The Gardener's Smile

Friends are beautiful flowers
In the garden of our lives,
Each one a different shape and hue
In the season when it thrives.

But they all have special purpose
In sharing their joy and grace,
And reminding us of the lovingkindness
In the smile on the Gardener's Face.

SJ Emmerson

Generosity is one thing, but selflessness is much more. Have I ever really been selfless? What are your prayers, poems, or ponderings?

80.

Today's Prayer

First

Matthew 6:33, Proverbs 8:17

Dear Jesus,

I praise You for this day. Every day is the day to seek You first. You stay close to those who seek You before all else. You are omniscient and know first-hand our needs and desires. You know what is best because You exist in the past, present, and future. Because You act from a love that reaches around all time and space, You will see that we get what is best for us even when we don't know what it always is. Lord, guide us carefully to keep You as our highest priority. Wake us up praying, praising, and studying Your Word. It is important to You, and vital to the quality of our lives.

In Your Name Above All names, I humbly pray-

April Roses

April roses with heads held high
Looking up toward evening's sky,
Lovely fragrance from times of old,
Calling out with voices bold.

Passerby stops to smile and praise
Considering more than a simple gaze,
Plucks a blossom's blushing face,
To give a gift of heartfelt grace.

God's blessing on its stem and off
A kind one's gain, the world's small loss,
But His Smile peaks through from up above,
To share with all some Light and Love.

SJ Emmerson

What am I putting before God? What are your prayers, poems, and ponderings?

81.

Today's Prayer

Gift Giving

1 Peter 4:10, Romans 12:6-8

Dear Jesus,

I praise You for this day. Today is another beautiful day in the lifelong season of giving good gifts to others. To some You have given the gift of serving, others may have been given the gift of teaching or encouraging. Generous giving is itself a gift. Leading others, showing mercy, and speaking Your Word are also gifts that some may have. The list of gifts is as diverse as Your list of believers. Whatever the gift might be, there is one essential rule for giving it. The real gift behind the gift giving season is giving it out of love. You literally wrote the book on that subject! Lord, thank You for all of Your good and perfect gifts. Please direct us, strengthen us, and enable us always to give out of the motivation of love. Remind us regularly that the season lasts all year.

In Your Name Above All names, I humbly pray-

The Gift of Giving

Giving is itself a gift
When the gift comes from the heart.
A silent, generous kind of gift
Holding another in high regard.

Giving is its own reward
Goodness comes to the generous
A favorite practice through Heavenly Eyes
When executed with tenderness.

Giving is a safe investment
Free from moth, theft, or flame
Paid back more than twice the measure
When God calls us home by name.

SJ Emmerson

What are my motivations when I share my gifts? What are your prayers, poems, and ponderings?

82.

Today's Prayer

First

Matthew 6:33, Proverbs 8:17

Dear Jesus,

I praise You for this day. Every day is the day to seek You first. You stay close to those who seek You before all else. As the One who is omniscient knows first-hand our needs and desires. You know what is best because You exist in the past, present, and future. Because You act from a love that reaches around all time and space, You will see that we get what is best for us even when we don't know what it always is. Lord, guide us carefully to keep You as our highest priority. Wake us up praying, praising, and studying Your Word. It is important to You, and vital to the quality of our lives.

In Your Name Above All names, I humbly pray-

Everyday Blessings

There are blessings in most everyday
In both the great things and the small
But for those who look for His Fingerprints
There is Goodness in it all.

The sunlight alone breathes back to life
Mother Earth and her offspring
Dressed in sunrise and sunset colors
And silhouettes of existing things.

One single, yellow daffodil
Sings in cheerful harmony
With aerial creatures and floating fowl
Snapshots of Nature's peace and tranquility.

Even the world we cannot see
Below us, above, and within
Teems with Exquisite purpose
Empirical evidence of a Divine Imprint.

One never needs to suffer doubt
That no Good will come his way
As long as we can draw a breath
There is a blessing in the day.

SJ Emmerson

What am I doing to show that I am demonstrating my love of God. Is this at the top of my priorities? What are your prayers, poems, and ponderings?

83.

Today's Prayer

Good Fruit

Matthew 7:16

Dear Jesus,

I praise You for this day, a day to nurture the good fruit bearing seeds that You have planted in our hearts. From Your tree grows good fruit, fruit that builds up our minds and spirits. Each bite of Your fruit is flavored with the sweetness of love. It is seasoned with joy and peace. Kindness, goodness, and faithfulness are perfectly blended into the multifaceted flavor. Finally, gentleness and self-control permeate all of the ingredients. These fruits are native to every country and come highly rated everywhere they are distributed. Lord, help us cultivate and freely share these fruits everywhere we go. They make excellent gifts separately or mixed together.

In Your Name Above All names, I humbly pray-

Special Treasures

To the world we may seem mundane
No different from the rest
But to God we're special treasures
Precious creatures loved and blessed.

He claimed us for His very own
By His Spirit through His Son
That we might become His children
Jewels polished to His perfection.

If you are treated otherwise
By our fallen, evil world
Remember you are a precious gem
God's priceless, dazzling pearl.

SJ Emmerson

Have I cultivated all of these fruits in my life? What is missing? What are your prayers, poems, and ponderings?

84.

Today's Prayer

Philadelphia

Hebrews 13:1

Dear Jesus,

I praise You for this day, a day to continue to love our neighbors as brothers and sisters just as You continue day in and day out to love us. Your tender care enables us to live out productive lives abounding in good things. Kindness, humility, joyfulness, peacefulness, thoughtfulness, and patience never lose their luster. They shine through the dingy, darkened clouds to add a bit of sunshine. You set an example, and we should follow it. Lord, keep us on the path of true righteousness. Even when we feel a bit lackluster, infuse us with Your warm, compassionate Light of brotherly love.

In Your Name Above All names, I humbly pray-

On The Day That God Made You

On the day that God made you
He only chose the best
Of strength and heart, and character
That would withstand life's difficult tests.

On the day that God made you
He chose kindness as a trait
That you have used in many ways
To build a life honorable and great.

On the day that God made you
He sent a star so bright
He made the world a better place
By sharing Heaven's grace and light.

SJ Emmerson

Was there any neighbor I left off of my "Philadelphia" list today? What are your prayers, poems, and ponderings?

85.

Today's Prayer

Jumping In

Psalm 94:19

Dear Jesus,

I praise You for this day, a day to find joy in everything. There may be, probably will be, some anxiety, but Your comforts will bring us joy. Your Presence will remind me that You never leave us because Your love endures forever. Your promises will ensure our restless minds that You have plans for a hopeful future for Your children. Your angels are guarding us, so why shouldn't we leap over our anxieties into some happiness today? Lord, thank You for all encouragement and every single opportunity for joy. Help us have the good sense to jump right on into it.

In Your Name Above All names, I humbly pray-

Bouncing Back

You may be down and out just now
But that is not where you have to stay.
You can always find the best of Help
When you bow your head to pray.

Such Aid may take a little while
There may be mountains you first must climb,
But come it will if you believe
A perfect answer at the perfect time.

So if things are looking grim at best
Because your life has veered off its track
Look up to where your Helper lives
And prepare to bounce right back.

SJ Emmerson

In what ways am I being encouraged? What are my strongest and weakest gifts? What prayers, poems, and ponderings do you have?

86.

Today's Prayer

Gift

1 Peter 4:10, Romans 12:6-8

Dear Jesus,

I praise You for this day. Today is another beautiful day in the lifelong season of giving good gifts to others. To some You have given the gift of serving, others may have been given the gift of teaching or encouraging. Generous giving is itself a gift. Leading others, showing mercy, and speaking Your Word are also gifts that some may have. The list of gifts is as diverse as Your list of believers. Whatever the gift might be, there is one essential rule for giving it. The real gift behind gift giving season is giving it out of love. You literally wrote the book on that subject! Lord, thank You for all of Your good and perfect gifts. Please direct us, strengthen us, and enable us always to give out of the motivation of love. Remind us regularly that the season lasts all year.

In Your Name Above All names, I humbly pray-

Encouragement

A soft, uplifting word or two
Voiced at the perfect time
Can mend a torn and tattered soul
To weave a lovely, new design.

Offering someone a helping hand
Converts a need into a gem
Energizing the weary one
To breathe and start again.

Just being near a grieving heart
Is rain in a desert land
It nourishes the seeds of hope
To grow in the wind tossed sand.

The language of encouragement
Is spoken in many forms
Each and every one of them
Has power to renew and transform.

SJ Emmerson

Who has been a source of encouragement to me in my life? What are some ways and who are the people I need to encourage? What are your prayers, poems, and ponderings?

87.

Today's Prayer

Great Grace

Ephesians 2: 8

Dear Jesus,

I praise You for this day, a day to celebrate the gift of Your Great Grace. We could never earn it; it is a gift given out of Your Love that knows no boundaries. The only thing we need to do is believe in You, the God of the only power in life that never dies. Lord of Love, may our neighbors see You in the grace we share with them. Guide us to be loving light bearers in a world with never enough. Help us to practice the fine art of a graceful giver everywhere we go.

In Your Name Above All names, I humbly pray-

The Gift of Time

Some gifts are given as an honor
To those we truly appreciate,
Such tributes show admiration
An atmosphere of goodwill they create.

Other gifts mark special occasions
Like birthdays celebrated with friends,
They serve as fond reminders
Of times we thought would never end.

There are many gifts of great value
Given from intentions purely sublime,
But nothing is more treasured
Than the cherished gift of a loved one's time.

SJ Emmerson

Who was someone who treated me with grace and love?
What are your prayers, poems, or ponderings?

88.

Today's Prayer

The Bottom Line

Romans 8:28

Dear Jesus,

I praise You for this day, a day to hold our heads up high and face both the joys and the challenges it brings with faith and optimism. When placed in God's Hands, our challenges are clouds used to rain on our lives and nourish God's good blessings. Lord, may Your Spirit tilt our heads upward and comfort our souls with Your joy. It is the best follow-up to the rain that sometimes falls from our eyes. Remind us to wear our shield of faith with assurance.

In Your Name Above All names, I humbly pray-

Climbing Uphill

No one ever claimed it was easy
To climb high upon a hill
It takes tremendous effort
Not to mention incredible skill.

One can become discouraged
As frustration rears an ugly head,
But we can stop and count our blessings
From the past and those still ahead.

Although we will have hills to climb
There is a Helper for such woe
He can surely aid us with such tasks
As He overcame them long ago.

SJ Emmerson

What challenges are causing me to lose my joy? What can I do to open the windows to God's positivity in those times? What prayers, poems, ponderings do you have?

89.

Today's Prayer

The Way

Psalm 16:11, John 3:16

Dear Jesus,

I praise You for this day, a day to be thankful for Your Great Grace that carries us from this life to the next. Because You exchanged Your life for our trip to eternity, we can rest in peace. We have been assured that there is a beautiful new chapter beyond the one we know here on Earth. You have planned for and created many magnificent opportunities for joy In this life, Lord. Only You and those who have gone before us know about the fullness of that joy we will discover on the other side. Thank You, Jesus, for the comfort of Your Lovingkindness and the promise of our heavenly chapters.

In Your Name Above All names, I humbly pray-

> What were some things I should be thankful for today? What are your prayers, poems, and ponderings?

My Thanksgiving

For pink and golden softness of autumn's evening sky,
For happiness twinkling in my children's eyes.
For time to hear the clock's clear tone on a quiet afternoon,
For a daisy's pixie dance and the rose's sweet perfume.
For welcome strength and laughter that friendship seems to bring,
For spring's cheerful morning song the feathered creatures sing.
For a mother's gentle kiss upon her baby's cheek,
For a father's stern protection of his child so mild.
For a room filled with the happy hearts of family and friends,
For unexpected messages of hope that Your angels send.
For an enthusiastic hug of a grandchild's waiting arms,
For God's unanticipated miracles that keep us safe from harm.
For the health and healing mercies extended by a Mighty Hand,
For courage, and peace, and hopefulness despite all of life's demands,
For ample opportunity to lift others up to You,
For those who have shown Your grace to me in ways both tried and true.
For breathing in the breath of life before my morning prayer,
For time spent with loved ones and all the memories we share.
For those who give much more to life than they will ever take away.
For kindness shown in countless ways that brightens the darkest day.
For new days and new journeys filled with joyful twists and turns,
For the year's fresh challenges that bring God's lessons of love to learn,
For the blessings of Your Spirit that feed our hearts and mind,
For those who demonstrate such blessings through actions loving,
generous, and kind.
For all the rich colors that You have painted into my life,
For showing me the light of Love within this world of strife . . .
I give thanks.

SJ Emmerson

90.

Today's Prayer

Lifted and Exalted

Isaiah 52:13, Philippians 2:9-11

Dear Jesus,

I praise You for this day, a day to commemorate the One who was both lifted up and exalted. Your coming was foretold centuries before Your arrival, but all that time You were preparing the way for us to accept You into our hearts. Knowing that You would be lifted up on a cross before You were lifted back up into Heaven, You still came to give us a real and lasting life. Lord, there really is no thanks generous enough for Your visit to our planet. The only thing personal enough is to give our hearts to the one who gave everything for us. Guide us to clear the clutter of our minds and hearts so that You can come close once again. I am very thankful to be back to this holy season and greet You once again.

In Your Name Above All names, I humbly pray-

The Star

Just like the Wise Men's guiding star
His Light will lead us through
The old familiar circumstances
And over the unfamiliar and the new.

We find it when we search it out
In His Word and in His Heart
In acts of lovingkindness
In genuine gestures of high regard.

After pausing for a humble prayer
We sometimes catch a glimpse
Of His dappled rays that part the clouds
As if we could touch His fingertips.

SJ Emmerson

What am I withholding from God in my heart? What prayers, poems, and ponderings do you have?

91.

Today's Prayer

Down in My Heart

Luke 2:10, Nehemiah 8:10

Dear Jesus,

I praise You for this day, a day to exercise the practice of joy. Unlike happiness that is a feeling that occurs when something positive happens, joy is an attitude that we adopt based on our belief in Your great goodness and grace. It is one of the choice fruits of Your Spirit. The joy of the angel's Good News the night of Your birth has never left us even if we have chosen to ignore it. Your joy is always there for the taking. Like Your love, we only need to open the door and allow it to come inside. Lord, Your joy is our strength. Grant us the ability to make joy as welcome in hateful times as well as the happy ones.

In Your Name Above All names, I humbly pray-

Finding Jesus

In the middle of the hustle
Of the Christmas holiday
We can easily forget the One
Whose birthday we celebrate.

We probably cannot find Him
When our nerves are frayed and stressed
Or when we are so exhausted
That our lives seem to be a mess.

Nonetheless, He has not left us
He loves us in spite of all the fuss
We can find him in the silence
Far away from all the rush.

SJ Emmerson

Which parts of my life make finding joy difficult? What are your prayers, poems, and ponderings?

92.

Today's Prayer

New Things

Isaiah 43:18-19, Romans 8:28

Dear Jesus,

I praise You for this day, a day to be filled with refreshed hope for the new things You are doing in our lives. The law of sin and death passed away when You came down to Earth and enlivened Your children with Heavenly Love and Light. Your Spirit has an incomprehensible way of bending darkness into light. The old might be gone, but the new has come. It comes not that we forget, but that we have hope for even more beauty in our days to come. Lord, help us to be thankful for the new things in life as well as the old. Sometimes, it is hard to move forward; but Your hope nudges us ever so gently on.

In Your Name Above All names, I humbly pray-

The Beauty of Christmas

The Christmas lights are twinkling
In the yards and on the roofs
Decorated trees bright and dazzling
The season's evidence beyond reproof.

Happy children watch with wonder
For signs of a certain sleigh
Many people bow their heads
To pray for peace on Christmas Day.

Friends and family gather
To celebrate with joy and cheer
Taking pleasure in the special company
Of those they hold as dear.

There's no need for acts of joy to end
Acts of faithful, caring hearts
It should be only a beginning
To a more beautiful New Year's start.

SJ Emmerson

What are some of the new things God is doing in my life?
What are your prayers, poems, and ponderings?

93.

Today's Prayer

New Things

Isaiah 43:18-19, Romans 8:28

Dear Jesus,

I praise You for this day, a day to be filled with refreshed hope for the new things You are doing in our lives. The law of sin and death passed away when You came down to Earth and enlivened Your children with Heavenly Love and Light. Your Spirit has an incomprehensible way of bending darkness into light as bright as the star that led the Wise Men to worship You. The old might be gone, but the new has come. It comes not that we forget, but that we have hope for even more beauty in our days to come. Lord, help us to be thankful for the new things in life as well as the old. Sometimes, it is hard to move forward; but Your hope nudges us ever so gently on.

In Your Name Above All names, I humbly pray-

The Beauty of Christmas

The Christmas lights are twinkling
In the yards and on the roofs
Decorated trees bright and dazzling
The season's evidence beyond reproof.

Happy children watch with wonder
For signs of a certain sleigh
Many people bow their heads
To pray for peace on Christmas Day.

Friends and family gather
To celebrate with joy and cheer
Taking pleasure in the special company
Of those they hold as dear.

There's no need for acts of joy to end
Acts of faithful, caring hearts
It should be only a beginning
To a more beautiful New Year's start.

SJ Emmerson

What are some of the new things God is doing in my life?
What are your prayers, poems, and ponderings?

94.

Today's Prayer

A Light in the Darkness

Romans 18:13, Revelation 22:5

Dear Jesus,

I praise You for this day, a day to soak up all of Your warm, bright rays of light that filter through the clouds of Earth. Your Lovingkindness cannot help but brighten all of our surroundings. You are the God of hope and happy tidings! We have much to anticipate through this season and every season to come because Your Spirit is most capable of flooding our hearts with the peace, joy, and hope of Heaven. Thank You, Jesus, for coming!

In Your Name Above All names, I humbly pray-

In the Corner

In the corner of my little house
Built in days gone by
Stands a tree aglow with twinkling lights
And hope on a desolate, winter's night.

On the front lawn of a lonely church
Once full of childhood mirth
Rests a manger centered with God's Own Heart
Declaring goodwill and peace on Earth.

In a hospital room where loved ones wait
For the touch of Heaven's Hand
A carol pierces the Silent Night
Accompanied by joy surprising and unplanned.

In a city struck by senseless hate
Where terror gives a vicious nod
His faithful angels watch over you
As heart-felt prayers are offered up to God.

Christmas comes to every place
No matter how dark or how small
As the Christ Child brings Light to the world
With a Love that is meant for all.

SJ Emmerson

What gives me hope? Joy? Peace? What are your prayers, poems, and ponderings?

95.

Today's Prayer

The Festival

Psalm 16:11, 36:8-9

Dear Jesus,

I praise You for this day, a day to attend Your festival that is going on in the hearts of believers. We don't need to buy tickets to anything to be in Your Presence which is the source of lasting joy. Believers only need to pray, worship, or study Your Word. In fact, anyone who loves has met You because that is what You are. Joy is a by-product of love. Lord, wherever we are and whatever we are doing keep us in close contact so that we may know the fullness of your joy.

In Your Name Above All names, I humbly pray-

Everyday Christmas

I never saw the mighty star
That marked the way to Jesus' birth,
But I feel His Light within my heart
Shining with joy and eternal worth.

I never heard the angel's voice
Singing of peace and goodwill to men,
But I've seen His transformational Grace
Renew my life again and again.

I never held the tiny Babe
Or gazed into the kindness of His eyes,
But He carried me on my darkest days
Replacing tears with a bright sunrise.

I never gave the Child a gift
Like the Wise Men of ancient days,
But I believe Him to be Heaven's King
Whose Forever Love is always a prayer away.

SJ Emmerson

How can I bring joy to someone today? What are your prayers, poems, and ponderings?

96.

Today's Prayer

Perfect Peace

Isaiah 26:3, John 16:33

Dear Jesus,

I praise You for this day, a day to be open our hearts and minds to Your peace. You are the Prince of Peace. Different from the world's offerings, Your peace is not contingent on circumstances. Rather, it is a gift of Your Spirit deposited directly into our souls. It is written that You will keep in peace those whose minds are filled with You. Lord, help us find Your peace each day even when it doesn't make sense-especially when it doesn't make sense.

In Your Name Above All names, I humbly pray-

The Good and Perfect Gift

The Good and Perfect Gift
Came down on Christmas Day
To bring us peace, joy, and love
That would never fade away.

He could have stayed in Heaven
At the right hand of God's throne
But instead He lay in a manger
Treasure for the poorest hearts to own.

He wore the Christ Child's body
And grew to be the Man
Who conquered evil on the Cross
Fulfilling His Father's holy plan.

The Good and Perfect Gift
Is given for all to receive
It is opened by a soul's whisper
"In His Gift, I do believe."
Wishing you His peace, joy, and love.

SJ Emmerson

When have I experienced peace that passes understanding?
What are your prayers, poems, and ponderings?

97.

Today's Prayer

In His Hand

Job 12:7-10

Dear Jesus,

I praise You for this day, a day to look and listen carefully to Your wisdom of Creation. They regularly teach us many lessons of life—the simple joys of the daisy smiling through cracks of the sidewalk, faithfulness of the sunflower following the sun, the love of a mother goose sitting on her eggs in a thunderstorm. Every living creature has a lesson to teach us if we pay close attention. They don't toil or fret as they know they are held in the Hand of their Father. Lord, grant us the faith of Your Creation.

I can only speak for myself, but I know I still have much to learn.

In Your Name Above All names, I humbly pray-

The Lily

Beside Christ's empty, open tomb
A flower bloomed on Easter day
Born again from Heaven's Light
That does not retreat or fade away.

Washed white as fallen winter snow
It humbly tilts Its head
Praying to the One Who lives
Souls' sustainer, our hearts' daily bread.

Grace-filled fragrance wraps the air
And lingers all around
Speaking highly of His hope and love
A silent presence most profound.

Lord, help us see Your story
In all of Heaven and on Earth
In simple acts of kindness
In every leaf's falling and rebirth.

SJ Emmerson

What faith points are evident in the world around me? What are your prayers, poems, and ponderings?

98.

Today's Prayer

Up and Over

Philippians 4:13, John 15:5

Dear Jesus,

I praise You for this day, a day to step up and over the obstacles that might block my love, peace, or joy. It is a day to move confidently into the areas You would have us move because You are the Provider who gives to us what we need when we need it. You are the One who is present in both good times as well as bad. You described Yourself as the vine that feeds, and we are the branches that must stay connected to grow and thrive. Lord, in every way on every day, send us signs of Your Presence. In every way on every day, please keep us connected to You. There are endless possibilities for us when we are attached to You.

In Your Name Above All names, I humbly pray-

What Greater Love?

What greater hope can we ever hold
Than the assurance of Heaven's home
Where the God of grace and mercy reigns
And welcomes His children as His own?

What greater joy can there ever be
Than to know Christ left His throne above
To replace the darkness in our hearts
With light and endless love?

What greater grace can be assigned
Than to open a hand to an angry fist
That He may lead us back to Heaven's home
And our transgressions be dismissed?

What greater Love can ever be
Than to endure hatred, shame, scorn
And hang upon a rugged cross
That our hearts might be reborn?

SJ Emmerson

Is there anything in my life that blocks God's presence in my life? What are your prayers, poems, and ponderings?

99.

Today's Prayer

This Day

Dear Jesus,

I praise You for this day, a day to be thankful for the patience You demonstrated with Your disciples as You prayed in Gethsemane. It is a day to be thankful for the incredible, daily patience You have exhibited so beautifully to us. You had to wake Your chosen disciples three times after You asked them to pray with you. You were literally sweating blood during this horrific time. It is a day to also be thankful for the fact, as well, that You were raised from the grave after three days. Father, Son, and Holy Spirit, help us remember to rejoice always, pray continually, and give thanks in all circumstances. Help us remember as well to wait at least three days for an answer to our prayers-just like You did. We still celebrate Your third day Victory as we celebrate the Divine Patience You have concerning Your children.

In Your Name Above All names, I humbly pray-

The Third Day

On the Friday that changed history
Even the rocks cried out
Those Who followed close to Him
Were shattered and scattered about.

The next day was a fearful day
A day of mournful doubt
One filled with nervous waiting
Dry hope and spiritual drought.

The third day was the turnaround
The Resurrection Day
The Bright Morning Star had risen
The Guiding Light, the Truth, and the Way.

SJ Emmerson

What things trigger me to lose my patience. What can I do to become more patient? What are your prayers, poems, and ponderings?

100.

Today's Prayer

A Special Freedom

2 Corinthians 3:17

Dear Jesus,

I praise You for this day, a day to give thanks and praise for the freedoms with which we have been gifted. The first one to consider is one gifted by You. Where Your Spirit is, there is freedom. We are free to communicate with You and open our hearts to You simply by believing. Your Spirit frees us from sin and death. Your children in the United States of America were given freedom from oppression over 200 years ago. We have more freedoms here than in any country in the world including the freedom to worship as we choose. Lord, we live with such great freedom as Your American children. Guide us to use it wisely. May we always be thankful for this invaluable freedom and remember to share Your Spirit through our words and especially by our actions. Bless all of Your children throughout the world.

In Your Name Above All names, I humbly pray-

The Unsung

Alone and in the face of fear
They tread on sacred ground
Where heroes sang a final song
But no one heard a sound.

Giving just because they care
They want no accolades
They only want to lend a hand
To God's child in need of aid.

They pray behind a private door
With a heart that God will hear
No other human soul is wise
To a prayer silent and sincere.

This type seems few and far between
But no one knows for sure
Only God can see into the heart
And find a spirit sweet and pure.

SJ Emmerson

How have my freedoms changed my life? What are your prayers, poems, and ponderings?

101.

Today's Prayer

New Things

Isaiah 43:16-19, 2 Corinthians 5:17

Dear Jesus,

I praise You for this day, a day to enthusiastically anticipate the new things You have in store for us. Whatever imperfections we run upon in this world of catastrophe and discord, we can always depend on You for new blessings in our lives. You have even replaced our old hearts with new ones. Lord, thank you for new beginnings and the new mercies that will accompany them. Remind us often of the old ones, too.

In Your Name Above All names, I humbly pray-

New Year, New Possibilities

The New Year brings new possibilities
To build bright and joyful days.
They are created with positive thinking
And forged by maintaining positive ways.

The New Year bears opportunities
For generating peace and not despair.
It is fabricated from our kindness
And through acts of thoughtful care.

The New Year yields fresh prospects
For living out our happiest lives.
The best ones begin with thankfulness
For blessings that enable us to thrive.

SJ Emmerson

What are some of the good things I anticipate this year?
What are your prayers, poems, and ponderings?

Prayers, Poems, Ponderings

Sandy Emmerson

1. What inspired you to become an author?
   My mother took me to the library when she went to check out books. She read to me daily as a child, and I have loved stories, poems, and the written word ever since. I recognized a need to write as a child, and I am thankful now that I have extra time to let the words out.

2. When did you first realize you had a passion for writing?
   I knew there was something that I needed to create as a young child, but I started writing poetry about eight years old.

3. What has been your biggest challenge as an author?
   Time to write is always my biggest challenge.

4. Who is your biggest writing inspiration?
   My mother, several encouraging teachers, and, overall, the love that comes from wonderful people placed in my life by a wonderful God.

5. What book are you reading right now?
   I read something in the Bible daily, and I am re-reading Norman Vincent Peale's biography along with other things.

6. What sets your book apart from others in the same genre?
   My coordinating poems, the opportunity for readers to respond with personal reactions, and, frankly, my "long range" perspective.

7. How do you beat writer's block?
   I need time and space to write.

8. What do you hope readers take away from your writing?
   I want them to be able to grow a little closer to God's Lovingkindness. I also want my readers to form their own prayers, ponderings, poems or anything else that results from reading the entries.

9. If you could describe your writing journey in three words, what would they be?
   Life-long, necessary, unearned

10. What advice would you give to aspiring authors?
    I would say to breathe out their words on paper as often as possible. The more they write, the easier it becomes.

11. What made you choose Lucid Books as your publishing partner?
    Someone I trust had attorneys check out the reliability of Lucid.

12. Where can we find you when you're not busy writing?
    I would be with my people sharing life, doing crafts, or reading at this point.

13. Where can we find you on social media/website?
    I have a Facebook and an Instagram page at this point.

About the Author

Sandra Jean Emmerson, Sandy, has been fortunate enough to see the best of more than one world. She has written about their lessons in both poetry and prose. Sandy has been a published author of poetry from a young age and has human interest stories published for a Texas based publication. After a long homemaking and stay at home mom career, her professional accomplishments include a B.A in Psychology and a M.Ed. as a Reading Specialist and Master Reading Teacher with certifications PreK-12th. She is a Certified Academic Language Therapist and a Licensed Dyslexia Therapist who has worked as a special education teacher, dyslexia therapist, literacy coach, district, regional, and state levels dyslexia coordinator, educational literacy consultant, and adjunct professor. She has many academic and professional awards and has collected a multitude of stories about God's Hand in all of it. Sandy is a proud mom of two beautiful daughters, Lacey Bavousett and Mycah Glover, grandmother (Sugar) to Emily and Gus, widow of her childhood sweetheart and husband Mike of 49 years, forever friend to the best people imaginable, and recipient of an unexpected, amazing muse named Robert. Future books include an illustrated collection of Nature's Wisdom, children's books, and an examination of Great Grace for a Small Town.

www.ingramcontent.com/pod-product-compliance
Lightning Source LLC
Chambersburg PA
CBHW060512090426
42735CB00011B/2193